"I highly recommend *Wit's End*. It offers great practical advice for parents who are struggling with an out-of-control teen. The book will help guide parents through the overwhelming process of finding a residential therapy program that fits their teens' needs. I recognize the importance of this book and will use it in my practice to assist parents when confronted with this big decision."

— Steffani Jaffe M.S., LMHC,
Child and Family Psychologists, Weston, Florida

"Sue Scheff's story is a story parents can learn from, and *Wit's End* offers hope, inspiration, and valuable resources for parents and professionals."

—Lorraine Colpitts, President,
Safe and Sound Transportation

"*Wit's End* is a priceless book for any parent or professional struggling with a troubled or at-risk teenager. It offers resources and information in a clear and concise way that will give people hope and inspiration when they feel helpless and alone. I highly recommend this book to anyone who works with today's kids."

—Terri Pardo, Parent

"Wow, what an amazing story of tragedy and triumph. Sue and her daughter, Ashlyn, are to be commended for sharing their stories and making such valiant efforts to help other struggling teens and their families. I recommend this incredibly helpful book to families with teens who need residential care."

—Dr. Gary E. Nelson, Author of
A Relentless Hope: Surviving the Storm of Teen Depression

"Sue Scheff's harrowing story brings hope, inspiration, and sound advice to people who care for teenagers and preteens."

—Gloria Pomerantz, Attorney at Law

"*Wit's End*, is an excellent read with solutions on an all-too-common parental problem. Sue Scheff invites us on her remarkable journey toward helping her teenage daughter, who was on the verge of serious trouble. Through her clear and tabulated prose, we learn why parents must demand accountability from any therapy given to their child. Scheff enlightens readers through her own tortuous experience and provides fifteen must-know points with detailed proactive solutions that parents can take when choosing which type of therapy and what therapeutic entity is the best for their child."

—John C. Fleming M.D., Author of
*Preventing Addiction: What Parents Must Know to Immunize
Their Kids Against Drug and Alcohol Addiction*

"*Wit's End* is a wonderful book that assists desperate parents in putting an end to their teens' destructive behaviors and damaging relationships to get back onto the road to success. Evaluating a variety of schools, programs, and residential and treatment facilities that are safe, effective, and qualified to provide the best assistance to facilitate and nurture the troubled teen, this book will turn pain and destructive chaos into emotional well-being and wholeness."

—Ruth Olmstead, Ph.D., Psychologist,
Associates in Behavioral Counseling

"All parents share the same awesome responsibility—to bring out the best in their children. *Wit's End* will help you do that by providing options and practical guidance for helping at-risk children. I highly recommend it."

—John C. France, M.Ed.,
Licensed Educational Psychologist

"When you are at the end of your wits, *Wit's End* is the place to start. Sue Scheff helps parents with at-risk children to feel more hopeful with her organization's motto, "Bringing families back together." She addresses various issues regarding the placement of troubled children and teens in residential treatment Programs and educates readers with a proven methodology of systematically evaluating the efficacy and effectiveness of each program or school being considered. As a licensed psychologist and a private and court-appointed family mediator certified by the Supreme Court of Florida, I strongly recommend *Wit's End* as a resource to assist parents and mental health professionals in locating the best residential treatment program to meet the needs of their child or teenager. No other book addresses these issues better than *Wit's End*."

—Dr. Mitch Spero, Licensed Psychologist, Director of Child &
Family Psychologists in Plantation and Weston, Florida

WIT'S END

Advice and Resources for Saving Your OUT-OF-CONTROL TEEN

Sue Scheff
Founder, Parents' Universal Resource Experts (P.U.R.E.)

Health Communications, Inc.
Deerfield Beach, Florida

www.hcibooks.com

Library of Congress Cataloging-in-Publication Data

Scheff, Sue.

Wit's end : advice and resources for saving your out-of-control teen /
Sue Scheff.

   p. cm.

   Includes index.

   ISBN-13: 978-0-7573-0697-6 (trade paper)

   ISBN-10: 0-7573-0697-7 (trade paper)

   1. Adolescent psychotherapy—Residential treatment. I. Title.

RJ503.S333 2008

616.89'140835—dc22

                                    2008008851

Publisher: Health Communications, Inc.

        3201 S.W. 15th Street

        Deerfield Beach, FL 33442-8190

Cover and interior design formatting by Lawna Patterson Oldfield

To my children, Ashlyn and Scott;
my granddaughter, Julia Sky;
my grandmother, Julia;
and my parents, Robert and Maureen.

In memory of my grandparents
(Guido, Maurice, and Stella) and
Donna Headricks—a very special friend
who was the original crusader for
the voices of the children.

Contents

Foreword

I magine that you're touring a remarkable set of caverns deep below the surface of the earth. Fascinated and captivated by the sights and wonderment around you, it isn't long before you wander off course—and only a little longer until you find yourself completely alone. You thought that you were following the right path, but somehow, mysteriously it seems, you can't find your way back. It's getting darker, colder, and more frightening by the moment, but as you frantically take turn after turn, looking for a way out, you realize you're only dropping deeper and deeper into the abyss. You call out loudly for help, but alas, no one responds. Will you ever find your way out? Anxiety and futility overwhelm you as a chilling realization strikes you: no one seems to know that you're lost, and even if they did, they wouldn't know how to help you.

Countless parents have found themselves in this very situation—metaphorically speaking, of course. Even the best and most cooperative adolescent can make parents question everything they've ever learned and believed, and when you have a teenager who's largely out of control, it may seem at times that nothing ever works, no one seems to have the answers, and there's no place for you to turn. It's not at all difficult to feel as if you're completely on your own—and you'd be right.

Sue Scheff took this bewildering and terrifying journey herself, along with her daughter, Ashlyn, and when no one had the answers, she figured them out on her own. When there was no place to turn, she searched until she found one, and when nothing seemed to work, she figured out why. Best of all, she's created detailed instructions and a veritable treasure map for everyone else—with the greatest reward waiting for those who follow it: a chance to repair their children's shattered lives, as well as their own.

In *Wit's End*, Sue takes readers on an amazing passage through the tortured adolescence that Ashlyn experienced, as well as the damage that can be inflicted by programs that make promises that they can't keep—and where therapy takes a backseat to bill-padding. If you make a mistake and place your teenager in the wrong program, the litany of horrors can be so extensive and so appalling that your child can be destroyed emotionally, while you can be kept busy facing almost certain financial devastation.

Rising from the smoke and ashes of her own experiences, Sue founded P.U.R.E. (Parents' Universal Resource Experts) to aid other parents in selecting the proper placement for their children. This extraordinary organization is singular in its ability to match children (and parents) with the facilities best suited to handle their needs. As a clinical psychologist in private practice, I've referred many dozens of families to P.U.R.E., and always with remarkable—even stunning—results. It is not at all an exaggeration to say that over the years, Sue has saved many lives, and as a result, she is revered by everyone who knows her.

Wit's End is the clearest, best-told, and most-riveting story of its kind ever written. From beginning to end, you will be caught up in a story so mesmerizing that it almost seems as if it must be fiction—but it's not. Travel through this superbly written and amazing story of the resurrection of lives, and you will be left bewildered by the idea that any one person can triumph over such overwhelming odds . . . again . . . and again . . . and again.

Sue has valiantly faced the most difficult imaginable circumstances and has prevailed each and every time. She had a troubled teenager, who is now a healthy, productive young adult. She removed her daughter from a horrifying program of systematic abuse and nurtured her back to health. She was the victim of a lawsuit that could have ruined her life, but it failed to have any such effect at all. She suffered a vicious Internet campaign that could have destroyed her credibility, but instead singlehandedly set a legal precedent in the area of Internet defamation. Sue Scheff is truly an American hero—and an inspiration to parents everywhere. Her tenacity, her courage, her dedication, her creativity, and her indefatigable work ethic will leave you in absolute awe—I promise you.

The next time that you feel as if you've gotten lost in the parenting morass and that no one can hear your cries for help, take comfort—Sue Scheff can hear you. She's listening, and, best of all, she has the answers that you're looking for. Sue Scheff can lead you back to the light.

—David A. Lustig, Ph.D., P.A.,

Licensed Psychologist, Private Practice,

Pembroke Pines, FL

www.gokoala.com

Acknowledgments

Acknowledgments

I don't know where to start since there are so many people who supported me in different ways at different times of this journey. First and foremost I have to thank my editor, Michele Matrisciani. There is only one word for her—*brilliant*—her creativity, support, and continuous dedication made this book possible. All authors should be as fortunate to have an editor so wonderful!

A special thanks to Heath Communications, Inc., and its vice president and publisher Tom Sand without whom this book would not be here. Thank you for believing in my story and wanting to be a voice for so many people and children who will benefit from this book.

A warm note of gratitude to the people who have contributed to my life and supported me through both the good times and the difficult times: Blanche Hardy,

John and Jaci France, Lee and Nancy Colburn, Jeff Berryman, Charlotte Greenbarg, Marie, Teresa C., Ann and Henry, Mark and Cheryl, Donna R., Cari D., Cathy and Russell, Leona, Joan and Bill, Lorraine, Eugene and Maya, Jim and Pat, Chris and Carol, Mary G., Diane and Rod, BK, Carol R., Michele and Jeff, Donna and Albert, Desi and John, Jill and Ed, Shane, Marion and Rod, Rick and Maryann, Terri P., Halli, Connie, and Nissa.

Finally, an *extra special thanks* to Jill Dahne, Norman Ratner, and Anthony F. Without these people I am not sure where my story would be.

Introduction

Perhaps you picked up this book because you are in a time of great stress and confusion over the state of your relationship with your teenaged son or daughter, and you can physically feel yourself being driven to the point of being at "wit's end." It is a feeling of hopelessness, helplessness, and complete isolation. You feel as though no one can possibly understand what you are going through. What happened to that happy-go-lucky, smiling, pleasant, athletic, joyful child you raised? Your teen is now acting out in ways you have always assumed only *other* people's teens act. "Not *my* child! You don't understand, *my* teen is so smart. I mean, very intelligent, and usually not like this. It is the *other* kids, not mine. Trust me, my kid doesn't do drugs." Yeah, I said that, too. "Oh, well, she only experimented once." You really want to make yourself believe it.

Has your teen become someone you don't recognize anymore? Is he or she controlling your household and causing you to feel held hostage to their behavior? Is your teen out-of-control, defiant, angry, rebellious, hateful, physically or verbally abusive, disrespectful, or more? Being a parent in denial can only make matters worse, while being an educated parent can help you recover the happy and innocent child you once knew. Seeking out this book is a great indication that you have already moved from denial to empowering yourself with the knowledge you need to save you and your child.

This book is divided into two sections and can be read in two different ways, according to your needs. You can, of course, read this book in the traditional way, from front to back. However, if the "frenzy" is upon you (and it is, if you understand the term), then you may turn first to Section Two, where you can focus upon the decisions that must be made about your child's immediate future and the options available for your making them. As soon as you have worked through that section, please return to Section One and follow my journey from desperation, helplessness, and hopelessness to learning the hard way what to do in the face of fighting for my child's life. I guarantee you, the more you become aware of the pitfalls that caught me, the more you will be prepared to avoid them yourself. You will save time, money, and emotional stress—enough to make a genuine difference for the better in your family's life.

After all, when parents or guardians are coping with an extreme case of uncontrollable behavior from a minor child, they are in a real predicament. In my and my daughter's case, our relationship had spiraled into something that I didn't even recognize. It went from parent *caring* for child to parent *fearing* her child, with an even greater fear that there was no way to turn back. I panicked. I had never experienced this type of defiance from her, and it was a new area of parenting for me. I couldn't find a parenting strategy for belligerence or a plan for diffusing her rebellion and verbal abuse. Add to that the fact that I was ashamed and embarrassed to share the stories of violence and unadulterated rage that my daughter was administering to me on a daily basis. I didn't know how to parent an oppositional, potentially dangerous child. But what I did know was that she was *my* child, and she deserved better than walking around in an explosive and obviously depressed haze. We all did.

As many do, I started with local resources to find the right therapist for Ashlyn and me. However, as you read our story, you will see that we climbed many mountains before we landed on solid ground. One of the first was learning to effectively navigate the new relationship that had evolved between us. For instance, for most of a child's life, the family has been rearing a young, more passive, and thus more guidable person. Now the family feels abruptly presented with a child whose uncontrollable anger propels them into violent or criminal actions. With the coming of the midteen years, a parent also faces a child who has recently become a capable physical adversary. It is during these teen years that a parent feels the time running out for an opportunity to use any genuine authority in guiding that child's life. Like me, you may not know where to turn to realign yourself and your child. I have learned the hard way how to do so, and through this book, I will share with you all that I've learned.

Residential Therapy:
A Viable Option

You should know right away that I strongly take the position—as controversial as some people find it to be—that when there is a serious crisis of teenaged behavior at home, then there is a positive place in society for Residential Therapy.

I know that many parents cringe at the thought of handing a child over to a group of hard-disciplined strangers. But I have personally witnessed many valid cases where such organizations have saved a teenaged minor from spiraling out of control and restored him or her to a productive personal life. At the time I was seeking outside assistance, I wish I had had the wherewithal and guidance to know that good places exist. Part of the reason I didn't possess this knowledge was because there is a "hush-hush" mentality parents take on in terms of whom they tell or share that they have lost control of their child. Ironically, it wasn't until years later that I discovered that several people I had known had gone through the same thing with their teens, and had sought out and found qualified and effective help through Residential Therapy. Unfortunately, this is a subject parents seem to be ashamed to talk about, so we don't know who to ask or who will admit they went through it, too. This is another reason I felt compelled to write this book: people need to share information to help others not to feel alone. How many news reports do we need to convince us that there is a disturbingly large segment of our youth population in desperate emotional and psychological need? Many are stuck in a loop of negative cause and effect because they lack the essential understandings of cooperation, fairness, and personal honor, which are offered and can be taught in Residential Therapy. This is the fundamental problem that *must* be fixed if they are to have a healthy life.

When you give birth to that precious bundle of joy, you would never dream in a million years that once adolescence hits, you will be considering sending them away. It just doesn't feel natural. The love for this child is so deep, and in the end, you realize it is this love that helps you take drastic steps. As parents, we have a responsibility to do what is best for our children, not what makes *us* feel best.

When Residential Therapy is administered by qualified staff who work under open supervision, it can and does save lives. Residential Therapy varies in settings, i.e., ranches, single-family homes, farm homes, lodges, or traditional boarding schools. But, in all cases, the setting should induce emotional support, accredited academics (where credits are transferable back to the children's schools), and a balanced combination of athletics, therapy, and social and life skills. In short, a qualified Residential Therapy program is one that takes children outside of their familiar setting and provides a positive, nurturing environment that helps children turn inward and receive a focus on emotional growth. In my work, I am less concerned about the type of physical setting that is chosen; it is *the program and its people* that matter most.

Saying "No" to Blame

As I mentioned before, blame has no place here, as far as pointing fingers toward why your child is in trouble. Sometimes the cause and effect of it is fairly obvious, but most often it's like trying to read tea leaves. I spent months, nights, days at the office, preoccupied and completely distraught over the "reasons" for Ashlyn's attitude and behavior. *It must be the lack of a father. No, it's my job. It is the friends she is hanging out with. She doesn't like her school. She doesn't like her teachers. She is depressed about a boy. I fed her the wrong foods as a child. I didn't breastfeed.*

For the purposes of this book, it simply does not matter why a child is in dire straits—whether you are responsible for any part of the child's struggle, whether you inherited someone else's problems, or whether the kid was just born under a witch's curse at the full moon. I wish I would've known this back then, when I was losing my daughter. Whenever a concerned parent/guardian of a minor child has decided that it is time to get professional intervention, then all that matters is that the child has an adult in his or her corner who can make realistic decisions with confidence. Originally, I didn't have confidence in the decisions I was making, so I want you to learn from my mistakes and discover what I now know about a parent's innate ability to make confident, well-thought-out decisions. All it takes is information and the serenity to process it into knowledge, and I am grateful for this opportunity to tell you everything I know to help you find the right path for you and your family. Reading this far is already so much more than I had done, so you are certainly on your way to saving your child.

It has taken years of personal experience and research to be able to confidently express the positions that I take today. There is no mystery to my point of view. It is simply the product of my personal journey with my two children, principally with my daughter, coupled with my current work as a parent advocate. I have carefully researched and observed many Residential Therapy organizations by running the Internet-based Parents' Universal Resource Experts (P.U.R.E.) to create parent awareness and provide safe and qualified resources for parents. Our driving focus is always to monitor and explore programs *especially* as they relate to the physical health and safety of children.

Overcoming Fears of Residential Therapy Programs

It is the minor child's essential safety that makes Residential Therapy a rational option for the responsible adult(s) in the household. Please notice that I use the term "Residential Therapy" in this book solely to describe those truly responsible and well-regulated schools and programs whose practices are objectively monitored, rather than programs that falsely advertise what they are providing and have limited, if any, credentials to operate a school or program. I had no idea that I needed to ask certain questions that I took for granted. For example, if you are sending your child to a Therapeutic Boarding School, you would "assume" their teachers are qualified and certified, wouldn't you? You would "assume" they have therapists. Unfortunately, you can't assume, and it's P.U.R.E.'s function to make aware to parents the programs that truly present valuable opportunities for families who are at risk of being shattered by the destructive behavior of a child in their home.

It is true that with some programs, there is a shock element. That is why the specific *method* is everything in a teen-help program. The places that P.U.R.E. recommends are all devoid of punishment-based structure. They are places of strict social and academic learning, within a framework of firm but fair restrictions that are placed upon all privileges unless cooperation is shown. They are not spas, but neither are they jails. They are places where all personal and social conduct is conducted under a firm set of rules based upon personal responsibility.

It is natural for any child who gets placed in an involuntary program to suffer initial feelings of shock and outrage once they realize where they are being taken. Most, however, will one day look back and see that they were in fact being thrown *a last and best lifeline*. And that it was a genuine act of loving concern, done by someone willing to fight to see that child make the transition into a young adult who can and will be a well-adjusted person, one who has a genuine chance of finding happiness in this life.

The worst cynics who comment on the topic of Residential Therapy tend to deride the parents who use it as being "too lazy or distracted to do the job of rearing a child." They portray such parents as using these programs for *de facto* teen-holding pens, and as a handy way to rationalize ridding the family of a thorny burden. As you will read later, I did question whether I was guilty of simply not being a "capable" parent, but the more I research and visit facilities, the more I realize I made the right call, just not at the right program. It was not about getting rid of my daughter; it was about giving her a second opportunity to succeed. As parents, we are our children's advocates. No one else is better qualified than us as their parents. As long as you remember this, there is no room for guilt. There is no time to question ourselves. Once we get past that, we can now help our children. Stop blaming yourself—and take action.

My years of experience have shown me that most parents who consider Residential Therapy are genuinely concerned people. There is nothing lazy or easy about the idea of sending one's child away. Quite the contrary. The caring people with whom I speak are just frightened and confused about how to help their child. Ironically, it is one of the parent's bravest moments.

In worst-case scenarios, I say that if a parent or parents are so unfeeling as to actually utilize Residential Therapy as a way to "warehouse" the child, then *that child needs the program even more*. There, at least, they will find more stability, more fairness, more acceptance of personal responsibility, and a deeper sense of personal value than they would ever experience otherwise.

Not All Programs Are Alike

However, Residential Therapy programs are also at the heart of a cautionary tale—there have been and continue to be appalling examples of profit-taking schemes that pose as disciplinary "camps" or "schools." Such places do little more than dump troubled children under the supervision of inexpensive and inadequately trained labor. Then they take away all of the kids' freedoms and their personal power, leaving them to languish under torturous conditions under the guise of "toughening them up." This leaves the already troubled child under the lash of whatever acts of abuse or foul temper the leaders choose to inflict. Since the child is the focus of the abuse, it is he or she who is most painfully aware of the fundamental injustice of their position. It's my belief that such programs pose a risk that any child who goes in angry will come out enraged.

There is an aspect of human nature that makes it possible for just about anyone to become monstrous, if they are given unmonitored power over dehumanized individuals. We don't have to go far to find it, not when an angry and frightened child is shoved into a plain wooden box and then left locked inside its stifling darkness over some meaningless infraction.

"Problem" kids who get stuck in such draconian places cannot only be expected to come back more troubled and angry but potentially also damaged in ways that may not be apparent on the surface. Such damage does not always reveal itself right away, either. They may, for a time, be frightened and beaten down into a state of compliance and submission that feels deceptively like good behavior to a parent or teacher. But the repressed rage will still be inside of the person holding it, and eventually it will make itself felt. As any victim of serious abuse already knows, people who are beaten into compliance may be passive and controllable for a while, but they are only biding their time to strike back, even if they don't know it. I witnessed the demoralization of my daughter after I made a last-ditch effort to save her. I made mistakes, and Ashlyn paid for them. Now my daughter and I are filled with the wisdom of hindsight that we hope you will be able to use in this critical time.

The Purpose of This Book

This knowledge I have gained through my experience with my daughter, as well as by talking with other parents of troubled teens and investigating treatment programs through P.U.R.E., has led to the wisdom you now hold in your hands. *Wit's End* will show you that:

• there are many treatment options available.

• you can competently evaluate the safety and effectiveness of various treatment options.

• you are not alone in the struggles your family is facing.

• your situation is not hopeless—there are viable alternatives to help your teen and your family.

• you are a good parent, capable of making these very important decisions for your child.

You have no time to waste. Read on to discover how you can get started in saving your child's life.

PART

ONE

HOW WE
GOT HERE

1

Our Story Begins

My journey to the knowledge that you will find in this book is the product of help from so many fine and caring people; I make no claim to have arrived here alone. I must also acknowledge that there is no way for me to impart this story without revealing a range of my own flaws. Some may seem familiar to you; others may not. Some I have overcome and left behind. Others I struggle with, even now.

I reveal these shortcomings for the purpose of assuring you that while we all struggle to do right, we also suffer the frustrations of failure in rearing our children. And if you should find that you recognize some of my mistakes in your own life, then I offer you both consolation and hope from one who has been there. I tell you that there is a way out for you and for your child, even if you are in that state of frenzy that I call being at "wit's end."

I started out completely ignorant about this entire part of the world. Until a parent is challenged beyond his or her ability to cope, why would anyone bother to learn about such places? Then one day I finally woke up to the fact that things had gotten very bad, frighteningly bad, between Ashlyn and me. She was almost fifteen then. Once I recognized that things were serious, I was off to the races like everybody else tends to be in that situation: at the library, on the Internet, on the phone, sifting for any information that I could use from any source that I thought I could trust.

Ashlyn is the eldest. My son Scott is the younger of the two. My initiation into the realm of Residential Therapy began with my own reactions to Ashlyn's changing behavior, but I also see in retrospect that much of her behavior at that time was not difficult to understand.

Here's a "spoiler" that I'm happy to give you early on: Ashlyn has emerged as a wonderful and responsible young adult woman today, with a good life and a bright future. She has contributed to the writing of this book and will be quoted on some of the issues, so please do not feel that you, as a reader, are violating her privacy in reading her story. She, like me, feels that an important part of our own evolution as individuals lies in using what we know to help others.

The Firestorm Ignites

Up until the time that Ashlyn reached the age of thirteen, she had always been a spirited and basically happy child, active and energetic. Ever since my divorce from her father, back when she was three years old, I had raised her as a single mother. She had no real memories of having a father around, and I thought that we had both done fairly well with our adjustment to life as a family. If she carried any big issues over the divorce, I had not seen them.

Her role in the story was thrust onto her while she was temporarily living with a family associated with her gymnastics trainer. Their home was near the gym four hours from our home, where she could train the maximum number of hours before and after school each day. She had been a gymnast and trained hard for years, and she had her sights set on a solid shot at the Olympic gymnastics team. Ashlyn was so dedicated that even after she suffered a terrible fall that badly fractured her foot and put her in a leg cast for six months, she stayed on the training schedule to do whatever work she could manage. It was a brave attempt to keep herself in reasonable shape until the cast finally came off. In spite of my concern for her, I was thrilled by her dedication; this was one kid who would not give up the Olympic dream without a serious fight. So she stayed on with the family near the gym to continue her training sessions.

In the meantime, I had met a man I'll call "Don," and we began to date. The house felt lonely with just Scott and me there. At first, things went so well—and truthfully, I had been alone for long enough—that I was willing to turn off my radar and rationalize away whatever signs he may have given that "long term" was not in the cards for me and Don.

I was too quick to turn off my powers of perception and fall into the wonderful feeling of a fresh romance. This mistake is a real sticking point for divorced women with children. I must confess that the prospect of having a whole family under one roof again was so magnetic to me that my better judgment lapsed.

Don and I became closer and closer as the months went by, and eventually we planned to try moving in together.

The prospect of living out of wedlock was less daunting than the thought of enduring another divorce. Without even bothering to check the online help manual, part of me was preparing for a negative outcome that my conscious mind had not yet even acknowledged.

And then, in a perfect storm of bad breaks, Ashlyn decided it was time to give up her gymnastics after all, following months of trying to work out with the cast. She felt time had just run out on her, since as her teammates continued moving up, she was stuck in her cast. She had to face the blunt fact that the recovery process had eaten up valuable practice time, which in her young mind could never be recovered. Despite all of her strength and persistence, she had fallen so far behind the other gymnasts that she felt there was no catching up.

This blow hit her just a few days before Don and I were to move in together. Still, I told myself that there could be a silver lining to this cloud, stuck as I was in denial of my own. This, I decided, could be a perfect opportunity for all of us to bond as a family. After all, Ashlyn and Don had spent enough time together over the weekends that she had come to feel comfortable with him. She was perfectly accepting of our relationship and of our living together.

But she was barely fourteen then and could not be expected to perceive things that I myself missed. Throughout my budding relationship with Don, she had only been home over the weekends, thus always a "visitor," not a daily family member. There was no real way for her to know what to expect.

Nevertheless, when it was time for her to come home for good, she appeared to interpret the new living situation as an opportunity. We both did. I was especially grateful to see that we had this new family to apply to Ashlyn's abiding sense of loss over her Olympic bid. She had come close enough to her dream to feel the brush of metal on her fingertips before her bones betrayed her and the golden ring passed by. The broken Olympic dream was an adult-sized emotional blow for her, but she and I both felt consoled over our new little family life.

It was in May when Ashlyn came back home to our new household and this next phase of our lives began. Barely two months later, the bill for my foolishness came due.

Don drained most of my bank account, kept most of my furniture, and threw us out. He did it just as abruptly as if he were only leaving me, and not the kids. The truth of my own complicity in this disaster hit me like a plunge into ice water.

My son weathered the whole thing much better than the women in his life. Our conflict was far enough outside of his range of concern that he was mostly able to ignore it. By August, the three of us had moved into an apartment, while I scrambled to support us and recover from being financially and emotionally wrecked.

However, as you might expect, Ashlyn was just as devastated over this rapid turn of events, although in her own way. She internalized this family grief and betrayal, somehow lumping it into her already bursting sense of loss over her gymnastics dreams while more adult-sized misery played itself out in her life.

This time, however, she had even less control over things than when she'd had her injury. Then, at least, she could make her own decision to apply every ounce of herself in the attempt. Here, the same spirit that carried her through months of workouts despite her cast now had nowhere to go in regard to this abandonment. She was paralyzed by the fact that this new pain had not been coming from her, but from the adults in her life. Life at home soon deteriorated until Ashlyn physically and emotionally retreated from us.

The details of the rapid collapse of my relationship with Don really don't have much to do with this story. We were still at the beginning when whatever sense of caution that my toe-in-the-water approach to domestic bliss was trying to express began to make itself felt. It was as if the sealing of the deal with our moving in together was the ignition point.

You know that feeling in the pit of your stomach, the one that appears when something is gravely wrong? It was there almost from the beginning. This family fantasy was not going to stand the reality test. And so those

two forlorn months were, for the most part, spent in bat-
tling the inevitable. I felt so foolish and so embarrassed
by my desperation in having allowed this situation that
I kept acting as if this thing was actually going to get
fixed. My passion in our arguments came strictly from
the blind hope that I was somehow going to talk us into
having the relationship we had both claimed to desire.
If I had stopped long enough to be honest with myself
about it, I would have had to immediately pack up and
leave. For awhile, the utter defeat in that was too awful
for me to confront. So I spent those two months in my
own form of denial. In retrospect, being in this relationship with Don was almost like being a parent who is
faced with a troubled teen; you keep hoping and praying
this awful situation will get better. You ignore the red
flags and all the gut feelings of "something is not right"
between the two of you, believing (hoping) it will get
better. As I swooshed away the crumbs that were left of
our relationship, I wasn't giving the children the attention they really needed and deserved. I was so stuck on
my making the mistake of moving in with someone that
I had a hard time focusing on anything else—or anyone
else. The feeling of making this mistake quickly turned

into feelings of guilt. I not only hurt myself, but I nearly destroyed my children. Even with their resilient nature, I stayed in this feeling of darkness and blame. While I felt sorry for myself and what I put my kids through, I didn't realize the serious impact it had on them, especially Ashlyn. It was the beginning of a roller-coaster ride that went on for a few years. By the time I emerged from my pity party, I realized Ashlyn had changed. I'm sure it was gradual, but it was too late. I was tardy in taking notice, and now she had gone to a place in which I didn't know how to help her.

The Situation Deteriorates

My kids and I started over in our temporary apartment, with me in an emotional tailspin that I should have seen coming but chose not to. For Ashlyn, this failed relationship, which in her mind was the chance to finally have a father, marked the beginning of our time in mother/daughter hell. Ashlyn lingered in a state of resentment and negativity, especially toward me, and it got worse by the day.

We both knew that I was the one who put her there.

Neither of us could escape the cold impact of my mistaken relationship upon our daily existence. Worse, it had been with a man she found likable, and with whom she hoped to have a good relationship of her own.

In the process of scrambling after all the details of that major shift in our lives, I quickly found that my own state of emotional shock made the routines that go along with moving feel completely overwhelming. It was embarrassing to find myself less and less capable with the mundane realities, but of course that did not keep them from happening. I was simply existing, giving my children what they needed, but not being there emotionally for them. I was emotionally detached, going through the motions of being a mother and provider, yet not being there. I ignored signs that I was losing my daughter while I was consumed with my own issues. Ashlyn started becoming very distant to me, whereas we were very close prior. She became secretive and started sneaking out of the house. At one point, she ran away for more than two days, which is one of the most frightening experiences a parent can go through. I called the police, who basically wrote her off as the "typical teen" and didn't take it seriously, in my opinion. I exhausted calling every one of Ashlyn's friends that I knew, even though Ashlyn's group of friends had changed. Finally, out of desperation, I called a local psychic to find her. I felt I had to do whatever it took, no matter what people thought of me. The world-renowned Jill Dahne lives in Hollywood, Florida, and I called her with my cry for help for my daughter. Within minutes, she was giving me ideas and her thoughts, and believe it or not, like you see on TV, she was right! She gave me a name that I wasn't familiar with, but after calling a friend, she knew exactly who this person was and Ashlyn was found. What infuriated me was that the parents of the child who had allowed Ashlyn to stay with them for more than two days didn't feel they should have called me.

From here, it just escalated to a completely foreign place. At first, I would receive calls from the school about her refusal to wear her uniform appropriately or to wear her ID, which seemed like very minor incidents, especially while I was in parent denial. But then I started learning that Ashlyn was skipping school and experimenting with marijuana and alcohol. She started dabbling in witchcraft and becoming a daughter I didn't recognize at all. I needed help. I was at "wit's end."

2

Getting Help for
Our Family

I n the new apartment, Ashlyn's frustration boiled
over into sheer outrage that increased with alarm-
ing speed. She began acting out in all the typical
ways available to contemporary teenagers. Most of it
was in the form of irritating but harmless rebellions of
fashion, grooming, and her choices of slang. But it was
also clear to me that this behavior was not enough to
flush the anger away. I could feel that the emotions boil-
ing inside of her were so powerful that they might move
her to strike out in more dangerous ways. It was all too

easy to picture her making mistakes in some uneasy frame of mind that her teenager's sense of immortality would prevent her from recognizing until it was too late.

That was the point where my depth of personal frenzy delivered me to the state of being at *my* wit's end. My own mistakes had been so toxic to my already injured child that she had completely shut down on me. Nothing I could do would get through to her. And, at that point, who could blame her? It must have seemed to her that the best way to survive was to do the opposite of everything I told her. Her behavior certainly made it look that way.

By the time that things decayed into constant troubles at school and frequent "runaways" for days at a time and ignoring her curfews when she was home, it became clear that I was not going to be able to prevent her from slipping further downward on my own. I was grateful that she had enough good sense not to involve herself with hard drugs, but it was a small consolation.

The final straw landed with her level of severe emotional reaction when she found out that I had been monitoring her computer use. This "invasion of privacy" caused her to go absolutely ballistic; she came at me with a knife. In my wildest dreams, I would never have imagined this. Ashlyn had never been an aggressive child; she was a fun-loving, happy child who loved gymnastics and Barbie dolls. I didn't know how to react or what to do. It is a moment in time in which you simply don't think; you just do what comes to you in that instant. I think that is what she did when she grabbed that knife. It was a moment of rage and anger I had never witnessed from her and never want to again. I was able to talk her down enough to avoid a tragedy, but at that point, the clock had run out on us. I was convinced that if I failed to act right away, something terrible was going to happen, and I had no power to prevent it myself.

Looking for Answers

I surfed the Internet, typing in key words, such as "teen rage," "teen help," "teen violence," "teen depression," "problem teens," "at-risk teens," "struggling teens," etc., to find teen-help programs. This was when I first became aware of Residential Therapy programs—and caught a major case of sticker shock at the prices they were demanding. As I was reading about the behavioral issues that these programs treated, I began to wonder what I was doing on these sites. *My daughter isn't like this*, I told myself, as I read about drug use, expulsion, violence, defiance, anger, disrespectful behavior, and so on. *Or is she?* Yes, that is the first realization you come to: your child is not the angel you thought she was, and you sit in shock that you are even considering this type of placement. Then reality sets in. *My daughter is really no different from the next at-risk teen, except that she is my child.*

Websites continued to pop up, containing jargon such as: *Are there changes in your child's friends? Are there changes in her appearance? Is your child running away? Is your child defiant? Does your child disrespect you? Is your child failing in school? Is she angry or violent? Can you trust your child? Is she sexually active? Do you suspect your child is using drugs? Do you feel your child is at risk? Troubled teen? . . . Difficult teen? . . . Struggling teen? . . . Problem teen?* YES! I could answer almost all of them affirmatively, much like when you watch a commercial checklist for the latest antianxiety drug. I struggled with contradicting thoughts and feelings, moving back and forth from total self-blame to resentment toward Ashlyn and then back again.

I continued my cramming session and discovered that there are different types of teen-help programs: Wilderness Programs, Therapeutic Boarding Schools, Residential Treatment Centers, Military Schools, Boot Camps, and more. How could I know what was best?

The teen-help business can be a powerful income-generator for unscrupulous operators, whose concerns stop at the bottom line and leave no room for respecting the well-being of those entrusted to them. If parents of at-risk teens are not aware of the lures that are used by fraudulent organizations, and if they are not informed on how to respond to them, there are legions of disasters waiting to snare them. Unsuspecting at the time, I further delved into the mysterious world of teen-help programs. The first such type I encountered was called an "Independent Educational Consultant."

This professional demanded $350 for an initial consultation, but I was not satisfied that the services warranted this kind of money, especially after I was told it would most likely be $3,500 to give me actual referrals to schools and programs. I had already taken Ashlyn to therapists, and I felt I could make the right decision for my daughter by finding schools and programs for her on my own, without paying someone that much money. Thus, I started learning about the variety of options available. (I have since become aware that Independent Educational Consultants can be extremely political, often recommending the same programs again and again with little regard for the individual teen's needs. I don't believe this is a time or a place for politics.) My first thought, which is common to many parents in my situation, was what about a Military School?

Exploring Options

There is a widespread misconception that military schools are modern-day reform schools, but that is not the case. A genuine **Military School** is an honorable place and a privilege to attend. To be admitted, most schools require prospective students to write an essay on why they want to attend that particular school. No student will be accepted if he or she is brought in dragging their heels. Rather, these schools seek motivated kids who want to focus on building excellence in their lives. Troublesome behavior only invites a quick dismissal and, in many instances, the forfeiture of your tuition. Therefore, parents should reject the idea of using a Military School as a threat to disobedient kids. It only results in a quick circle of negative behavior and punitive consequences and puts you right back where you began. Easily dismissing Military Schools as an option for Ashlyn, I continued my search.

The sort of organization that I was trying to find was one that would provide therapy through some form of internal self-examination that would be guided by qualified professionals. What I learned at the time was that these types of places are called **Specialty Schools**. My research on behalf of Ashlyn made it clear that many of these programs and schools are operated under the auspices of the World Wide Association of Specialty Programs (W.W.A.S.P.). Their stamp of approval was meant to indicate meaningful standards, so I focused my search among their member businesses. It seemed that W.W.A.S.P. was the giant in the industry of "teen-help." They advertised parent seminars and posted testimonials from parents that could have been my own story. I felt like they were definitely what I was looking for. In desperation and quiet hope, I requested more information to be mailed to me. After receiving W.W.A.S.P.'s literature, videos, and parent references, I decided to choose one of their programs nearest my location: Carolina Springs Academy.

When I wrote to them for a brochure, they sent four identical PR kits by postal mail. To this day, I don't know if that was a dumb processing mistake, or a clever marketing tactic to create a sense of urgency and get you to actually open one of the packages. I could also assume it was to share them with family members, our therapist, or even Ashlyn's teachers.

It was a package of beautiful glossy literature and an accompanying video that would make any frightened parent weep. Carolina Springs Academy boasted a therapeutic setting with horses (Ashlyn loves horses), and a guarantee that Ashlyn would make positive changes by the time she graduated the program. If she didn't, she could go back at no cost for sixty days. By the time I had gone over all of it, I was beginning to feel hopeful. It also seemed like a special blessing that the cost of the program was less than some of the others and had their no-cost guarantee. This sounded really promising, and with the sales representatives telling me how children graduated the programs in as little as six months, I figured that since my child wasn't "that bad," she'd be done within that time frame or soon thereafter.

This place seemed to combine the no-nonsense environment that I was certain Ashlyn required with a truly therapeutic environment. They offered private psychological counseling to those who need it. This was an extra cost, however, at $100 per session, which I found out about later.

As I understood the school's overall message, it was simple—today's spoiled kids live in a cocoon, convinced that they will be rescued from any unpleasant situation by whatever adult is responsible for them. The Academy assured me that everything they did was calculated to impress upon each "student" that during this time, in this place, they were going to have to rescue themselves. A weakness or fault that might prevent any one of them from progressing would have to be fixed solely by each individual, and any failure to address it would negatively impact the entire group. This was the sure-fire way to impress upon each individual a clear concept of interpersonal loyalty, to teach them social responsibility.

It sounded like a possible answer. So with a deep sense of dread still in my stomach, I called several of the "parent references" the Academy provided. They each gave glowing reports of success. (Shortly after I enrolled Ashlyn, I attended the first parent seminar in which we learned, among other things, how to "sell" the program and gain a free month's tuition. If your child already graduated, you would get $1,000. I felt this was a great way not only to have tuition paid for but also to share this "wonderful" program with other parents who are struggling. It simply didn't occur to me that the Academy would use shills, or use their seminar to turn me into one, but client desperation is a seller's greatest ally.)

The dread did not go away when I began to seriously consider enrolling Ashlyn, but at that point I did not trust my own emotions very much. I felt so lost, so alone, and it just didn't feel natural to send her so far away from me while we were so disconnected already. Ashlyn had grown so distant from me . . . would sending her farther away help? Not completely sold yet, I did as the Academy suggested and attended a members' support group, where I could meet and hear from parents of children in the program and from parents of graduates. Being around these satisfied parents who really understood my situation gave me the confidence to go into check-writing mode. I had made my decision: I would enroll Ashlyn.

Ashlyn Enters the Academy

When you have an explosive and potentially violent child, many places recommend bringing her in under a guise, so that she doesn't have an opportunity to get physical and attempt to run away in panic. I had no idea what I would do if Ashlyn did become violent or run off in her determination not to go, so I went along with the Academy's suggestion, telling her that she was going to attend a "traditional boarding school." She was quite willing to go along with that, ready for anything to get out of the house. It was my hope that she would eventually realize that I was doing the best I could for her.

Once Ashlyn was at Carolina Springs Academy, it was my turn to hold up my part of the bargain. As a parent of a child enrolled in the Academy, I was required to attend mandatory "seminars" for parents and caregivers.

At that first seminar in Ft. Lauderdale, Florida, about three weeks after Ashlyn had gone, I found the behavior of the seminar representatives to be odd.

These "continuing seminars," in my opinion, turned out to be long, self-serving propaganda sessions. They were aimed squarely at keeping parents convinced that their kids had to remain in the program for the full duration to achieve lasting benefit. They drilled into us to "trust the program," and whatever you do, they instructed, don't pull your child until she is "fully baked." They used this term quite frequently, and it felt insensitive to me. Being at the "seminars" was like attending a convention of ditto-heads and feeling intimidated from questioning their processes. My natural cynicism protected me from being caught up in the crowd hypnosis, however. I never fell for their continual pitches for an increased duration of membership for our kids. Plenty of other parents seemed to take it all in. Maybe those other parents who attended were all sincere, and perhaps none were "seeded" into the audience as paid enthusiasts. I don't know for sure, but as a group they certainly behaved that way. I found the intensity of the ditto-head atmosphere among them to be suffocating.

The students at the Carolina Springs Academy and many other such places are assigned "Levels," according to how well they are deemed to be absorbing the program. Ashlyn was a Level 2 throughout her entire duration at the Academy, which kept her under a strict program of isolation from family and friends, stripping away all familiar support. This meant that she was never allowed to call me, and I could not speak to her. The sales rep's mumbo jumbo grew repetitive, but the clear message coming out of the Academy from the moment that I let Ashlyn walk in there was that they needed to be left alone to work their magic.

Hidden Costs

Ancillary costs began to add up like grocery receipts once I enrolled Ashlyn in the program. As soon as we arrived to drop her off, they immediately asked, "Where's her uniform fee?" Their first question about her, right up front, was a plainspoken statement of their priorities. It would be verified again and again.

After she disappeared into the Academy, Ashlyn remained isolated and out of touch while I prayed that intelligent discipline and group rapport would help her rebuild her self-esteem and come to terms with her anger. Understandable as that anger was, I hated to see it persist any longer than it needed to and hoped that she could adapt a healthier manner of living than I had demonstrated to her.

I eventually learned that the parent seminars were so successful in their persuasion and recruitment pitches that some of the children were left in their program for *two to three years*. After a thousand days, the parents paying the average $400 daily tuition rate would have moved $400,000 into the program's bank account—even if they managed to dodge the pressure to go for "extra fee" services and sign up for "program upgrades."

It also became apparent that many of the programs show a pattern of keeping kids completely cut off from the outside world for at least the first six months. I learned this through an online parent bulletin board system (BBS), where many parents divulged to me that their kids were in the program well over a year. *In many cases, it can take up to a full year before the parents are allowed to see them.* On this BBS, I learned that several kids from Carolina Springs Academy were rushed by ambulance to the local hospital for food poisoning. I started questioning this since my daughter was there. When I spoke with one parent directly, she said her daughter was in the hospital, and she was flying to South Carolina to get her. She asked me if Ashlyn was one of the kids who got sick, and honestly, I didn't know. I said she must not have been since I didn't hear anything from the school. Wouldn't they let me know? I called and left a message for my Family Representative. Several days (and many messages) later, I heard from her. Yes, my daughter had been taken in, and no one had told me! That same day, I received a letter from Ashlyn telling me how sick she was and how she had gone through the ordeal alone! No one had told me about this.

As fast as I could, I pulled Ashlyn out after that first six months, no matter what kind of excuses the Academy fed me. In spite of my sense of guilt and my own self-recriminations over helping to make it necessary for her to be there, a little wad of dread never fully left me.

After I got Ashlyn back home, I was hit with the highest of all the hidden costs: the trauma inflicted upon her at Carolina Springs Academy. Ashlyn was so determined to never return to that place that she was filled with suicidal thoughts of what she would do if ordered to go back. It was not teenaged melodrama on her part. As her story unraveled, I began to understand exactly what she meant.

3

Ashlyn's Story

*S*even years after my daughter Ashlyn's term at the Carolina Springs Academy, this is what she says about her experiences there.

I went willingly to a place that my mom had presented to me in brochures. To me, it looked like a regular boarding school with activities, sports, and horseback riding. However, upon arrival, I found that the place was nothing like the pictures I was shown. The admissions process was enough to throw me into a tailspin, and I threw a fit shortly after the staff went through my belongings and stripped me of all my things, including my makeup, underwear, hair accessories, and jewelry. The scare tactics and intimidation started the moment that my mother wasn't around anymore. They never got better.

They ran me through the process of getting a uniform, but there was no orientation and no explanation of the rules. It was nearly impossible to ask anybody to help me understand what was happening, because a strict rule of silence was enforced. If you were seen simply asking another kid how something was supposed to work, you would draw punishment down on yourself and probably onto them, too. That first day went by in a blur that still hasn't completely cleared up for me, and I suppose that's just as well. I felt like I was living in a dream that was quickly turning into a nightmare. The only information I got was from watching everybody else and trying to go along with things. The staff members seemed like hovering attack dogs, all looking for an excuse to strike. The slightest infraction was an invitation for severe punishment. The staff would stare us down, waiting for one of us to turn our heads, cross our legs, or speak to one another, to bring us down a level.

By the start of the second day, the numbness of the first day began to wear off, which exposed me to even more reality than I could handle. I woke up from my dream state—or maybe it's better to say that the initial shock wore off, you know, the "Welcome to Hell" shock. The staff had plenty of other shocks stored up and ready, even though I didn't know that yet, and they could shock you pretty badly anytime they wanted. I found out that much right away.

It happened just when I was already beginning to boil over with this sense of being trapped in some kind of place where things were going way beyond just strongly enforcing a bunch of rules. The whole atmosphere of the place felt *wrong*—and if there were any actual rules that the staff was working by, other than "no talking," they weren't made known to us until we had broken them. It was as if they were only there to frighten and bully the other prisoners, and I use that word intentionally. It was pretty clear to me early on that calling us anything else in that place was a joke.

The main structure where we were held was like a triple-wide trailer building. It was small enough that the staff had no problem telling where any problems might be happening. So, partly because I was new and wandering around ignorantly, and partly because I didn't think twice about jumping into somebody's face if they seemed to need it, I wandered into my first really useless conflict with the Academy's authority.

I was talking to this girl, whom I will call Nicole, and she seemed all right to me, but a few minutes later I heard her fall and saw that she had just collapsed. Right away, she started going into these twitching convulsions. I had never seen anything like that, just right out in the open that way. But the most amazing thing was that nobody moved. The kids looked scared or at least interested for a little bit. Then they either stood by as if nothing was going on at all, or they went on about their business.

I could see that there were staff members around, close enough at least that they should know what was happening. But either they weren't paying any attention at all, or else they knew that Nicole was in trouble and they just didn't feel like dealing with it. The only thing I knew about CPR then was what I'd seen on TV, which seemed to involve yelling for somebody to do something "stat"! So I wasn't going to be able to help her myself, but there was no doubt that she was in real trouble.

When I finally got to a staff member, she just acted all busy while I tried to tell her that a girl seriously needed help. She frowned and looked annoyed at being bothered. Then she told me to just "hold on" and went about her business—as if this was a complaint about the food. By that point, I was so amazed and frustrated that I could hardly get any words out.

"Shut up" happened to be one of my hot buttons. Okay, she didn't say it in words, but she said it loud and clear with attitude. That really set me off, so I started yelling—maybe *screaming* is the word, depending on your point of view. I was dropping f-bombs, calling them all f'ing freaks, demanding help for Nicole.

My antics and attempts to call attention to Nicole's state were such a severe infraction that they stuck me into Observation Placement (OP) for the next seventeen hours. OP can best be described as an isolation box, which the kids renamed "ISO boxes," set up outside with no windows, no heat, and no air conditioning. When they put me in, they told me that to win my release, I was supposed to use the pen and paper they provided and write an essay. It was supposed to explain the details of why I was wrong.

I started out writing essays that they would send back and tell me to do over because I insisted that they had no right to treat anybody as they had treated Nicole or me. It was a good performance by my tough-cookie persona, but I had never had to hold it up for so long. Eventually, after hours of dueling over words, I finally wrote what they wanted to see. My forced confession included that I was sorry for my screaming. I should have raised my hand, and my terrible actions made the situation worse than what it was. By the seventeenth hour, this seemed like the right choice to make.

Survival Mode Kicks In

Over that stretch of hours, I discovered that even a small amount of isolation can be extremely powerful. That's all the more true when you have no way of knowing when your isolation will end, and when there is no way to predict what will happen next. This instinctive fear comes over you. It hits you like a blast of heat. Nothing that you tell yourself has any effect. Your brain can jabber away about staying calm, but it doesn't matter. My admission of guilt was the beginning of my survival and coping mechanisms at the Academy. I decided that I had to fake it to make it. Do, act, and say whatever the program wants, no matter how much I went against my basic instincts. I tried to write letters to let my mother and others know what was happening, but the program convinced the parents that what the letters say are just devices of manipulation and should be ignored.

They did finally get an ambulance for Nicole, and she fortunately survived. This was good news for everybody, all the way around, since parents tend to stop sending checks after their kids die.

The truth is that I had some pretty clear ideas about why my mother had stuck me in that place, even if I was strongly opposed to being there. Still, even though I realized that she had her reasons for being so upset and fearful, nothing that I was seeing in this place made sense to me—unless the entire purpose of the Academy was simply to provide cruel amusements for the staff.

At fifteen, I didn't see the money part, although I learned about it later. I knew that my mom was spending money she couldn't really afford for me to be there. But I never totaled up what each one of us kids was worth to the place, or what a whole bunch of us might be worth. I suppose a lot of what went on would have been easier to understand if I had been sophisticated enough to see it as a matter of pumping the most money out of the parents while spending as little as possible on the kids themselves. A lot of their justifications about the general crappiness of the place would have made a lot more sense to me in that light.

I eventually found out that the working philosophy there, if you want to call it that, was to break the individual down as much as possible. You're easier to fix that way.

It makes more sense if you think of it as being like cooking up a tough piece of meat—first, you stick it with a fork a couple of hundred times, so that it comes out nice and tender. I was today's meat. One day earlier, I had been feeling pretty tough, for a fifteen-year-old girl. But today it was already clear that the only way to make it around this place was to tolerate it while they stabbed you so many times that you finally got tenderized enough that you lost your toughness. They wanted their kids tender enough to cut with a spoon.

The next day consisted mostly of learning how to tell the staffers the right lies to get them to leave me alone, at least for a little while. My fake cooperation got me out of the isolation cubicle, but they still kept me under general observation for the next couple of weeks. Back with the general population, I took a bunk bed with about sixteen other girls in one room. We didn't have windows and our rooms smelled of urine, mostly because the bathroom toilets were always overflowing. Meeting the girls, I learned what they were "in" for. The reasons varied: drugs, prostitution, being raped, being molested and beaten by family members, being sexually active, among other reasons.

Daily Life at the Academy

Our typical day went something like this:

• 7:00 AM: wake up, make bed.

• Work out to video while staff laughs at us.

• Breakfast (could be a small bowl of cereal or four pieces of bread).

• After breakfast, we'd march to another building that was called "school." There was no structure to our day, no lessons. We were on our own, but could put our name on a list for a teacher's help if we needed it.

- Lunch (could be a pizza pocket, four pieces of bread, peanut butter and jelly, or turkey and cheese, depending on the day).

- March back to school.

- Physical education: Consisted of our marching back and forth. On our lucky days, we might get to play kickball.

- Dinner: Listen to motivational tape and write three things that we can learn from it. I never really paid attention. Food was generally the same thing we had for lunch.

Twice a week we had group sessions, which were facilitated by a staff member with no therapeutic qualifications. We were often called "whores" and "victims" during these sessions. Bible study was offered once a week, but was promptly removed, which we assumed was because the Academy realized we actually enjoyed it.

If we didn't have group, we would watch a video about drug use or write letters home.

Afterward, we'd shower, straighten up the area, and go to sleep.

Starting off my stay by branding myself as a trouble-maker was, possibly, not the smartest move. The extra focus that it turned on me was not the kind of attention that anybody would want. The staff collectively decided that I was a rich, spoiled princess. They nicknamed me "Daddy's Girl" and jeered at me for ending up in such a place. They assured me that I was there because my soft "Daddy's Girl" lifestyle had ruined me, causing me to expect my life to be handed to me on a platter. All of my objectionable behavior was the result of my attempts to throw a tantrum at the world and get what I want from Daddy again, just like always.

It was especially ironic and bitter for me to hear that, since I'd never had a "Daddy" at all. And "rich" was not a word that anybody would use to describe my mom, my brother, and me. But those little differences were just not things that mattered here. They would have only mattered in a place that was genuinely dedi-cated to helping every person who goes through the program. Instead, it was a handy form of shorthand for them to write me off as a whining brat. When I tried to object, I found that everything I said was immediately dismissed as either another whine or an outright lie. Unless I said whatever it was that the staff wanted to hear at any given time, anything else I said was dismissed as merely aimed at getting myself some advantage that I did not deserve. When I tried to deny that, my "contrariness" was then simply labeled as being proof that they were right about me.

As for the rest of the program, I won't bore you with the routine stuff, the constant screaming in your face, the physical assaults with tackling and pinning if you were slow to respond to orders. It all just boils down to their system of six "Levels" of rank, based on your staff evaluations. The idea was for a kid to aim as high on the number scale as possible to have any privileges at all. To be allowed any direct contact with the outside world, you needed a Level 4 or 5. It was *extremely* difficult to move beyond the level that was assigned to you.

I made it to a rank of Level 2 and stayed at Level 2 for the entire time I was there.

At that Level, I was not allowed outside communication or any visits at all, even from my mom. I could send letters, but even then, the staff would read them first and would either physically censor them or call the parents to warn them that the manipulative letters we had just mailed were "inventing stories" to help us get home. The parents were allowed to know as little as possible about what was really happening there.

In my case, they told my mother, for example, that a manipulative kid like me could be expected to invent all sorts of terrible stories, just to try to play on my mother's emotions and buy my way out.

It was perfect—how could I deny being a liar? By the time that all this came crashing down, I had gotten pretty good at lying to my mom, or any other adult, just to keep them at bay.

But from inside of this place, when I begged my mom to believe me, I was perfectly cast as the girl who had cried wolf too many times to be believed. The casual lies that I once told at home, just to cover my tracks, now made it easy for my mom to believe the Academy's story that I was just inventing things about the place to benefit myself.

At that time, the scariest thing was that it was so

clear that the Academy had developed a perfect way to enforce secrecy, by using our own past behavior to knock us down. It was this weird form of invisible judo, and it felt just as powerful as the blunt physical shock of having a staffer shove you onto a sofa or into a wall.

Living in Unreality

For the whole time I was there, it was always totally unreal to think that any place like that actually existed. No matter what anyone might say about the descriptions of behavior that the kids wrote home about, many of the things in my letters could have been easily checked out by a parent's visit. Any parent who paid a surprise visit and really snooped around would have seen the wooden punishment boxes right out behind the girls' dorm. They would have had to wonder what the things were for. But the staff had cut off that danger by tripping us over our own past behavior.

At night, it was like being a prisoner in some third world country. I could hear screams coming from the girls locked inside those boxes. You could hear a lot by listening to the particular sound of their screams. Some of the girls might have just been crazy, screaming in anger at the world. But, of course, there were stories about rapes. You never knew. The thing is, it didn't matter if the rape rumors were true or not for the fear factor to work on you. You lie there, and your imagination gets going, whether you want it to or not.

Sometimes I would lie there and think about Jamaica. The word was that the Academy had another location in Jamaica (called Tranquility Bay), and it supposedly made this place look like a day camp. I tried not to imagine being stuck in one of those wooden "punishment boxes" out in that jungle heat and humidity. At least in this country, there had to be some fear of the law to slow them down.

But what kind of laws would they have for protecting kids in a place like Jamaica? None of us knew the answer. But everybody went on the assumption that whatever the laws were in that place, they didn't mean much. Runaways, it was assumed, disappeared off to Jamaica if they caused "serious" trouble.

For each of us, Jamaica conjured private images of a dreadful, faraway place. We all realized that whatever went on in Jamaica, it was surely something much worse than the asylum already surrounding us. We could only speculate. That was something nobody really wanted to do, but none of us could avoid it. Not me, anyway. Not lying there at night in the darkness and the enforced silence, listening to the muffled screams from within those punishment boxes out in the back.

You wind up thinking weird things, like wondering if those screams would sound different in Jamaican. A girl I was friendly with got sent there. I never heard anything from her after that.

As much as I objected to this place, I also realized that I had put my mom between a rock and a hard place with my behavior. Still, it felt as if I had been sent to Death Row for it. It seemed unbelievable that she could truly be aware of what went on there. I had no idea what they might have told her, but my instincts told me that she could not possibly have heard the truth from these people. She would have been here. No matter how mad I had made her, I simply could not believe that she was knowingly cooperating with this parade of bullies.

The group sessions consisted of repeated episodes of personal humiliation in front of the others. We were forced to sit on the ground and pound the dirt with our fists until the skin was broken and bleeding. This was supposed to help us get rid of our anger. It was amazing, though, how quickly the throbbing in your hand bones and the cuts in the skin made the anger build right back up.

We were also taught to visualize the effects of our bad choices by acting out improvised scenes of our own execution, complete with being shot to death. This was done with open glee from the staff members, who went after the process as if they were settling old personal scores with the kids themselves.

We had to stand up in front of the group and come up with a list of the people who would want to bother attending the funeral of someone as "bad" as each of us, who had lived the way we had, causing the sort of trouble that we had done to find ourselves there at the Academy. Any positive effect that might have resulted from the enforced internal reflection was canceled out by the open pleasure that the staff appeared to take in their "duty" to break us down. I had no sense of being helped. There was a strong sense of being trapped and under a constant state of threat.

It got worse whenever something went wrong with the place itself, like with the plumbing. The sewage pipes clogged all the time, sometimes backing the toilet up onto the floor. The staff didn't bother to clean it, and none of the staff would issue any cleaning supplies to us. It was policy, they said, to avoid allowing any of us to get access to the dangers of suicide by poison. Eventually, the wet sewage soaked into the carpet that lined the floor of the sleeping room. It made the place smell like a public outhouse.

At fifteen, I was old enough to appreciate how ironic it was that a motive for suicide by poison was seriously raised by their refusal to allow us any cleaning supplies to get us out of that disgusting environment. I was pretty sure that with some more fresh air in the place, a lot of those suicidal urges would tend to go away on their own.

The only time we were encouraged/ordered to clean everything up was just before a new family arrived that was considering placing their child at the Academy. It was nice for the place to have a clean surface appearance for a little while, but many of the actual problems never got fixed. Pretty soon, everything went back to the way it was. Sometimes it made me feel sick just to think about the kind of health hazards that were lurking in that foul smell and the damp carpeting.

Sure enough, before my time there was over, the fouled environment eventually did more than just advertise its potential for contaminating us. It contaminated our food. A traveling food poison rolled through the group, eventually taking us down with severe stomach pains and overwhelmed immune systems. My dose hit me so hard that it seemed to shut down every organ that I didn't need to use for moment-to-moment survival.

The staff response moved at the usual turtle pace. By the time that anything was done to help us, my vision had blurred and left me temporarily blinded. Eventually, all of us were rushed by ambulance to the hospital emergency room. Eventually, everyone got their systems cleaned up enough to get well again. As we recovered, one by one, they took us all straight back to the Academy.

Nobody ever contacted my mom about any of this. She remained completely unaware of any health difficulties with me for the entire six months of my incarceration there. Once again, because of my low Level assignment, there was no way for me to get to her with the truth.

After all, the staff kept each kid at the lowest possible

Level, because that's where they had the most control over you. At the low Levels, they could be certain that there was no way for you, as a prisoner, to fight back or to get any outside help. It helped to justify keeping a kid in the program for extra months, until she or he was finally judged to be a true Level 6 *(Properly Tenderized, Falling Off the Bone—Fully Baked).*

You could get out sooner, though, if your family went broke.

It wasn't until after my mom showed up and pulled me out of there that I also learned to consider the Academy's strong financial motive for slapping kids with low Level evaluations. For me, the nastiest part of that revelation was the thought of all that money flowing through the place—and they couldn't see their way clear to *fix the plumbing?*

Getting Out

By the time I left (escaped, was how it felt), I was in such a state of despair and depression that the impact of being back in the outside world was a real blow of its own. By this point, it seemed as if I had forgotten most of what I knew about who I was supposed to be. I knew that I wanted to lead a better life and to build better relationships, but I didn't know how to trust my own judgment anymore. I felt angry with my mom, even though I could understand her position, and I was as mad as hell about the place itself.

After getting out, daily life felt more like a series of little blows that seemed to come out of just about anything that I did, or any place I went. The smallest complications or obstacles became invisible wires that I tripped over, again and again. The adjustment was such a radical effort that my mom and I had to seek therapy in helping me reenter what was left of my old life and to begin rebuilding a new one. You can bet that I felt angry and resentful of her when I first got out. But the more I learned about the tricks that they had played on her, the more I began to feel angry for both of us.

It was a long process, sort of like untangling a giant ball of knotted string, one knot at a time. Oddly enough, it was partly through the process that my mom and I discovered how much we have in common—both of us *really* want to strike back against irresponsible specialty programs. We completely agree that neither of us should walk away from the task.

Today, years afterward, I am married and a new mom. I have worked for some time with a wonderful school whose efforts work on behalf of troubled teens. Everything that we do has the individual health and well-being of each child as our prime concern. And every time that I see that policy carried out, I also know that it is another blow in a long series of blows we are delivering to *any* abusive Residential Therapy program that seeks to profit on the backs of troubled families and fails to give adequate regard to the welfare of their clients. We will keep the message out there that there are honest, healthy alternatives available that have already been checked out by other parents themselves.

People can tell me that I was only put into that place because I was such an angry and self-destructive teenager. But I can tell you that I came out as angry as I went in. The difference at the end was that they gave me a direction in which to focus that anger—toward them—and a strong motive to fight back. With my therapist, my mom and I were able to work through our mutual feelings of hurt and betrayal, but nothing would ever make that place and its practices be okay with either of us. To me, the idea of turning the other cheek, in this situation, would have only felt like a complete surrender to those bizarre and hostile practices.

It turned out to be very bad news for W.W.A.S.P. and for any other organization that dares to approach teen-help as a profit-taking scheme, because they are the ones who made warriors out of us. Both my mom and I have committed to a continuing battle that we cannot consider walking away from, not any time soon.

Together, we simply acknowledge it is the right thing to do.

4

The Aftermath

Hi, it's Sue again. If you are a parent, I don't need to tell you how shocked I was to learn about the things that had happened to Ashlyn, as well as mortified to realize how I had let them play me. My first reaction was to be more worried about her than ever, fearing that I had only managed to deepen her problems. Once I could see that she realized that we had both been victims of a hoax, I felt an inkling of hope that we could somehow repair this. Then I was mostly furious with myself for not having followed up on those urges to drop in and see how things were going, no matter what the staffers had told me about their "accepted procedures."

I had not trusted myself enough to follow up on my instincts, fearing that my interference would jeopardize the program's process. Ashlyn's experience there was the price paid for that mistake. In a sense, the Academy reps were telling the truth, because if I had pulled a drop-in visit at the Academy, my arrival would have "jeopardized" the place, all right. I would have immediately tried to get them closed down.

Alone with Ashlyn in the wake of all this, I felt like a bomb had gone off in the room. Both of us were floored by the stories that we were confirming back and forth. We each experienced cascading realizations of how many different levels of trust these people had violated. I could see Ashlyn alternating between flashes of anger at me and the staff. But neither of us experienced any drop in our need to do something meaningful—something within the law, but still something with teeth—about these torture programs masking themselves as therapeutic environments.

Maybe the Academy's biggest mistake was in underestimating the power of the mother/child bond (once the two stop screaming at each other). When that mother and child discover they share a common threat—and it is a big, grinning thug of a threat—they each become more incensed over the other's plight than they would be over their own. And so the former conflict between them is reversed into mutual cooperation, and then that energy is boosted by the relief they both feel for being able to drop the interpersonal struggle and be free of its stress. That freed energy is added to their considerable common resource and then focused upon the offender, where mother and child have no reason to restrain any of their outrage.

The Academy must have expected their game to keep working for them, as such things always had. Nevertheless, they had made it impossible for Ashlyn and me to walk away licking our wounds. I could feel the power of the trauma that they had pumped into her with their unceasing mind games. In her sleep, she seemed to spend most of her time fighting terrible nightmares. She would sometimes jolt awake with a cry.

Her depression was strong when she first came home. She radiated a strange and unusual form of stillness that was troubling to see. Almost sixteen at that point, Ashlyn had always been a bright and energetic girl. For years, her youthful exuberance had been beautifully channeled into her gymnastics, and her health was superb. Even back when she had been acting out at her worst, she still exuded better self-esteem than this. Someone had taken the damage that my choices had inflicted upon her and carved them deeper into her, all under the guise of "therapy."

There was no time to dwell on my mistakes, with so much to be done in the here and now. There was no magic to the work; we just kept talking. To Ashlyn's credit, she started talking several months after being released from the Academy, instead of retreating behind a teenager's impenetrable shell. If she had closed me out then, or run away from home, it could have destroyed both of us. Instead, I am so proud of her. Ashlyn never lost her willingness to believe that her flawed mother made her best efforts to understand and address her problems. That goes for the ones that her mother caused herself as well as for the ones she did not.

We had a lot of mutual gaps to fill over that six-month time frame, so the curtains were pulled back one layer at a time. Rather than having a single "Ah-ha!"

moment, we found ourselves having a long series of them.

They say that what does not kill us makes us stronger. No thanks to the angst inflicted on Ashlyn in that place, she had indeed grown stronger in the meantime. I began to witness it, in spite of her depleted condition, in the form of her persistence in working out the truth of what had happened to her, and in the fact that she was charitable enough in her bruised spirit to also care how the long fiasco had affected me.

So we talked and we talked, and the closer we came to a common vision of all of the facts, considered from both sides of the story, the closer we came together between ourselves. It was a poignant and beautiful process that left me stunned with gratitude. We had somehow managed to convert this disaster into a second chance for us, which meant that it was a second chance for her, no matter what else happened. It felt as if we had been fighting off attackers at the front and the back of our house, and in the meantime this miracle wiggled its way down the chimney.

Striking Back

I might have been able to swallow their manipulation and dishonesty if it had only been directed at me. But after what they had put Ashlyn through—while assuring me that she was doing well in a safe and sane program—I had to react with all of my energy. She was just sixteen and needed to focus on taking care of herself. Shortly after Ashlyn returned from the Academy, I founded Parents' Universal Resource Experts (P.U.R.E.) to aid any parent in need of qualified placement for their at-risk teenager. At this time, I wasn't sure where this was going, but I wanted to help other parents who were in my shoes. Our organization was composed of parents who individually and collectively take the time to investigate and report back to us on all sorts of programs. In many instances, we get feedback from parents and students from a variety of programs of their firsthand experiences that we can pass on to the next parent looking at that particular program. It is about parents helping parents and sharing information. Their input is vital to the process of keeping us updated with the most current information possible and allows us to make a range of fine adjustments to whatever program or programs are recommended to each specific family. This is important because each dynamic between a parent and their child is unique, requiring its own solution to problems that are undoubtedly longstanding and complex.

In furthering that work, I set up a website for P.U.R.E., and later a series of websites, each geared for disseminating the information about today's teens and parenting as they relate to different issues. On the initial P.U.R.E. website, I told visitors the same story that I told here about the W.W.A.S.P.-affiliated Carolina Springs Academy. I left out Ashlyn's first-person story at that time because the events were still fresh for her.

And then, because of those statements on my site—which were provable truths—W.W.A.S.P. sued me, saying that I was supposedly a "competing business" who was defaming them to "get their clients." What was I supposed to do with the business I "stole" from them? This absurd allegation was a puzzle, because my little freelance endeavor was not connected to any school or program at all. P.U.R.E. is an organization to create parent awareness in an industry that is new to them. As a parent of a teen who was at risk, that feeling of desperation and isolation can lead to rash decisions. P.U.R.E offers helpful hints when you enter this teen-help arena, as well as offers alternatives we have personally visited.

Further, they called my comments on the site slanderous of them. What was probably most upsetting to them were the stories my daughter and others were telling about their "time" in the W.W.A.S.P. facilities. One story recounted a boy who was literally put into a dog cage and made to lie on his stomach for hours on end. There was another account of a boy who had his elbow dislocated by a staff member, and yet another, by a girl who had her jaw dislocated by a staff member. To compound this, *48 Hours, Dateline,* and *Primetime* exposed this alleged abuse and obvious neglect of children. Ashlyn's story was bad, but compared to what other victims of W.W.A.S.P. had endured, she was one of the fortunate ones. By posting my daughter's account of her time in Carolina Springs, I hoped her story would prompt parents to look deeper and find the other more horrific incidents.

But as everybody in this country knows, anyone here can sue anyone else. The idea of that sounds fair enough, at first—until you take into account that when a large business or a wealthy individual threatens to sue, there is virtually no actual impact upon them as the complaining party, whether they win or lose. They are playing with house money. Their lifestyles will be unaffected; their homes will not be lost; their careers will not be shattered.

On the other hand, for any person, and especially a single mother of limited means, the threat of a corporate lawsuit means the specter of being forced into bankruptcy, regardless of right and wrong. The moneyed party can issue a continuing stream of baseless motions and further charges, drawing out the lawsuit's time and expense to levels that are ruinous for the defendant.

Of course, I was painfully aware that if their ridiculous charges prevailed, I would be wrecked in my fledgling career, and my mission to clean up residency programs for kids would be over. I was still raw with bitterness over what they had done to my daughter and to many other kids, and especially over what they proposed to keep right on doing in the future.

Their plan was to come at me with enormous, vague, and nebulous charges whose potential for protracted litigation would intimidate me into a quick settlement.

A settlement would have required me to take down my websites and to forever keep quiet about what I know. I am convinced that it never seriously occurred to them to wonder if I might hesitate to settle with them. They must have been operating their case on autopilot. There would ordinarily be no way for anyone in my position to fight back, so they clearly considered my retreat from the truth to be a done deal.

The capacity for anger is a two-sided coin, of course. I have cost myself enough with it in the past to know better than to give in to its influence, unless there is severe provocation. It's just that this particular provocation was that outrageous. It was as if I could no longer swallow, or even draw a full breath, until I got busy fighting back. There was just no way that their accusations and threats could be acceptable.

While fighting back was difficult, it would've been a lot harder if I hadn't had my little ace in the hole. Nearly two years earlier, a wonderful friend had badgered me into buying business insurance to cover my entrepreneurial efforts, and I eventually relented. The policy cost me about five hundred dollars a year, which had only totaled about a thousand dollars so far, and it protected me from just this kind of malicious lawsuit.

I sought out an attorney named Richard Henriksen in Salt Lake City, who was highly recommended to me by a friend. While Richard was a plaintiff's attorney, his deep compassion for children and their safety compelled him to gladly make an exception to defend me, once he heard the story of my being sued by a massive organization like the W.W.A.S.P.

For the first time in a long time, I felt a real ray of hope. Despite what would ordinarily be a terrifying situation bringing the prospect of financial ruin and public humiliation, I found myself with the ability to fight back—along with a tough and knowledgeable attorney to defend me. The plaintiffs also sued my colleague, Jeff Berryman, who is a good and well-intended person who was only helping to spread the word about the dangers of poorly monitored programs under W.W.A.S.P.'s oversight. To his credit, Jeff also refused to accept an intimidation settlement. Instead, he retained my same attorney and settled in for a fight.

Going to Trial

I'll spare you the details of the lawsuit. The entire
case is on public record for anyone who wants the
blow-by-blow version. Here it is with all the boring
parts filtered out:

I defeated W.W.A.S.P. in a jury trial. The case ended
with the supreme Court of Appeals upholding the judgment in my favor. I, indeed, had the right to share our
story and continue P.U.R.E., which shares accounts
from others.

Over the course of that long flurry of legal action,
and in addition to the grueling discovery process and
the hostile depositions, the attorneys for W.W.A.S.P.,
in a last-ditch effort to incriminate me, obtained cor-
respondence between a W.W.A.S.P. parent and me. She
had sold it to W.W.A.S.P. for a sum of $12,500, but in
the end, it was deemed useless by attorneys for both
sides. The W.W.A.S.P. parent then went out on an
active Internet campaign to smear me. I never learned
if she was being paid for that part of it, but her persistent attacks had a strong sense of driving motiva-
tion that I could not understand. I was certainly not

aware of anything between the two of us that seemed to justify her attacks. Still, they accelerated until she openly accused me of being a con artist, a fraud, and a crook. Of course, for anyone like me, who hopes to guide others to the safest ways to help their troubled children, this level of defamation was so intense that I had to hire a separate lawyer in Florida, David Pollack, to formally challenge it. The trouble with any kind of concerted smear campaign is that if the victim remains silent long enough, then the very lack of comment is interpreted as some form of an affirmation of the charges. Any individual or organization requiring credibility with the general public, and especially with their client base, can find themselves in very troubled waters if someone targets them for an Internet gossip campaign.

My position on both sides of that argument has brought me to the belief that everyone has a free forum on the Internet, but because of the random public exposure afforded to any posting on any site, the line between negative opinion and reckless name-calling and slander has to be respected by everyone. That fundamental awareness of one's own conduct while on the

Internet is every bit as essential as it is for us to demand that everyone who drives on the public roads must know how to read the road signs and obey them.

Free speech has never included the "right" to inflict slander or libel.

I took action and sued the woman for Internet Defamation and Invasion of Privacy—and won. I was awarded damages by a jury in the amount of $11,300,000 (eleven million, three hundred thousand dollars). It also set a new legal precedent in support of the right of free speech on the Internet. It did nothing to give people power to slander one another; it simply locked in the right of free speech in the Internet forum when you want to speak the truth.

Furthermore, while the impression of anonymity spurs many users to make statements and adopt attitudes that they would ordinarily not assume in public, the wake-up call greeting some of the more vicious public attack-mongers today is that your ISP number (your computer's unique address) is tracked everywhere you go, just as visible as footprints in fresh snow. It just *feels* anonymous because you can use it alone, adopt a screen name, even fake an entire Internet persona, if you have the need and lack the conscience. But any one of us is *always* only a single formal investigation away from having their ISP ordered from their server, identifying their specific computer by name and location.

Knock, knock, knock. . . . What's that? Oh, just a sheriff's deputy at the door with a subpoena for you.

At the time, there were some Internet postings making wry comments about me, to the effect that this woman was "only doing the same thing" to me that "I did to" W.W.A.S.P. The singular difference, however, was that what I had to say were provable truths, while the postings about me were nothing but invented accusations/speculations. I only felt so confident in my position because I knew that they could never prove their claims and that clearly this was their last-ditch effort to shut me up, thus keeping their tactics a secret, especially in the light of my winning the original defamation suit they brought against me. However, this now meant I had voluntarily placed my life at the center of two simultaneous lawsuits. You don't need a law degree to know how dangerous that is. Even though both of them felt absolutely inevitable to me, it made for a terrifying prospect. Both were in reaction to vicious verbal attacks that were being made in such widespread public venues that if I failed to respond in a strong fashion, silence would be construed as a confession. The damage would also go far beyond my own defeat, affecting every one of the families in crisis who would no longer have access to the information that P.U.R.E. made available.

The good news is that the W.W.A.S.P. lawsuit ground its way into court . . . and died there. It was squashed by my brilliant attorney and a host of parent victims who spoke on the witness stand. The simple fact is that they accused me of slandering them, but the larger fact is that the truth is considered a perfect defense against any charge of slander. In other words, they had to offer a specific example of slander from me, and they had nothing. They hated to hear what I said about them, but every word of it was researched and reflected the plain truth.

I was vindicated of having unlawfully damaged their company in any way. P.U.R.E. had always prechecked the advice and warnings that I said on my sites and still does.

Whatever "damage" we were doing to them was nothing more than the direct consequence of their own actions. Their lawyers couldn't hide that.

It is a real comment on our current media's sense of priorities, though, that this verdict denying all W.W.A.S.P.'s claims—this failure of corporate intimidation of an individual over the right of free speech— received only moderate attention. Never mind the effects upon countless young people and their families all over the country. Instead, the verdict that received the most media notice by far was in the suit I had to file to stop that woman from working so hard to defame me on the Internet.

Regarding that judgment of $11.3 million, $5 million of it consists of an additional penalty that was levied against her because of the sheer maliciousness of her actions.

This case set legal precedence on the topic of Internet Defamation, and it is now part of our legal system's attempt to catch up with the evolution of personal media and Internet communication. I am glad for the needed precedent, but it was my vindication after being sued by the W.W.A.S.P., and the affirmation of First Amendment rights, that was far more important to society and to our kids. Today, well-moneyed bullies cannot safely attempt to bolster their bottom line and silence the flow of valid knowledge by using attack-lawsuits to force suppression of the truth. It has become fiercely dangerous for them to attempt to silence vital public warnings, and justifiably so.

The big money verdict was far less sweeping in its legal effect. But it did put another brick in the growing civil firewall that is intended to protect the reputations of innocent people from attacks by "Internet flamers." The phenomenon of online flaming is especially troublesome because it can seep onto the Internet from so many different sources, whether those sources are motivated by profit, by the pursuit of personal revenge, or by that random form of crazy hostility that thrives on the Internet and, particularly, the blogosphere.

Victory

After the second trial was over, the jurors waited in the hall, where they hugged me and told me to please continue my work on behalf of children and families. They told me how moved they felt by what P.U.R.E. does, and that they recognized the need for it. They did this after hearing the testimony of five witnesses, who showed the extent of the damage that this malicious lawsuit had done to everyone working with P.U.R.E., and especially to every one of the families who did not get the support from us that they needed—and which we could have otherwise afforded to them if not for the time and expense of that legal action—because of the consuming nature of this lawsuit. The witness group included a psychologist, who confirmed that he had to stop sending parents to us because of the ugly allegations posted on the Internet.

In the wake of the second verdict, I received a rash of e-mails and phone calls from victims of Internet defamation. I had never realized that it was so widespread. All these people had been smeared in Internet blogs. So while this verdict isn't exactly the legacy I pictured for my kids, I am still proud to have survived it and to have endured its challenges.

I had learned the same painful lesson that anybody who gets targeted in a lawsuit tends to learn: it will find every doubt or point of insecurity that you have and place it under a magnifying glass, in your own eyes. You will lose time from countless other obligations and pleasures in life while you huddle with an attorney or sit in on yet another procedural hearing.

Privately, you will go back over everything, straining to be certain that you are not leaving out any details, distorting any facts, or mistaking one thing for another. That's the cancerous nature of the thing. Even when the court system works as it should and an innocent person is exonerated, there is no form of compensation for the creeping waste of time and energy that will have been expended. Even the victor walks away damaged.

For Ashlyn and me, the long process eventually strengthened our relationship because it emphasized our growing common bond in our determination to get rid of human warehouses that pose as "programs" for troubled teens. I don't intend to minimize our personal struggle just because I'm not treating it as some kind of tabloid drama. We each have demons to battle, and we both struggle to keep them out of our relationship with one another. It's just that we have so much more working for us today.

In mid-November 2006, the woman who inflicted an Internet smear campaign against me located a lawyer who attempted to set aside the judgment. The rich irony of this lawyer's involvement in the case is that he normally advocates for teens who are abused in such programs! The attempt failed, and the entire $11.3 million judgment was upheld on my behalf.

Do you wonder if I will ever collect? The answer is . . . probably not the entire amount, but there will be collections. As for the W.W.A.S.P. case, even though they lost against me legally, they have persisted with an Internet blogging campaign, issuing "warnings" about me and my organization. We would assume they know better than to use falsehood against me now, so they have been hoping to score with implications and anonymous postings. In response, I retained a team of professionals, Reputation Defender (www.reputation defender.com), who specialize in keeping your online reputation clean. This ugly campaign will eventually pass away, too, like the others. In the meantime, there is so much work to do.

I finally feel whole again. I am able to enjoy daily life in a way that I haven't done in years. But I do think that until you go through the legal system—all the way through a jury trial—it's difficult to imagine the levels on which the struggle affects you. It makes an impact upon so many different aspects of your life that it can almost turn you into a different person. Sometimes today, I find myself speaking in a more cautious and deliberate manner than I once did. I don't mean in the sense of social manners and the use of tact; I mean sheer self-censorship with an eye to steering around sources of potential conflict. I suppose that's a good thing—a safer thing, at least.

It's inevitable, though. In going through a lawsuit, you learn more than you ever wanted to know about the law. Afterward, there is always that little demon of fear sitting on your shoulder, ready to ask if whatever sort of wrongdoing that concerns you at the moment is *really* worth turning your life upside down for. Nearly always, of course, the answer must be a prudent "no."

It's just that sometimes, no matter what we would prefer, the answer is a solid punch in the face that says "yes." There are few enough personal boundaries left in our society, and interpersonal respect has nearly disappeared in the public arena. No matter how carefully we maneuver in the marketplace, we are subject to its culture of unenlightened self-interest. And so we will, whether we care to or not, either absorb a long series of random drubbings without serious protest, or from time to precious time we will suit up, stretch out, and fight back.

There is nothing to glamorize in the process of doing that, either. Like so many blunt facts of life, it is a long exercise in patience and persistence. Those late-night pacing sessions can really eat a hole in the carpet. The anxiety can really eat a hole in your stomach. The frustration and anger can really eat a hole in your heart. And, insurance or not, the lost work time will absolutely eat a hole in your bank account, one way or another.

I know the truth of that, having been to that place, and having escaped by the narrowest of margins. It's just that I also know how fine it is to fight back with a bully and win.

PART

TWO

How You Can
Take Action

5

Choosing the Program
That Best Fits
Your Child's Needs

T his is the Action Section of the book. It is written
for you. You have a problem with your child that
is too serious to be ignored. Here is how your
options break down.

1. **Local Therapy.** If you have not yet tried individual counseling and/or group therapy for your
   teen, this really must be your first stop in dealing
   with out-of-control behavior. We assume that
   your child's behavior is of such concern to you

that you have bypassed "light-touch" approaches, like having a relative or teacher give her a pep talk. The situation is beyond anything that your cleric, if you have one, can minister away.

You may have tried arranging a visit to a jail for your teen, a personal "scared straight" move on your part. Those things can work, temporarily, but what about the root causes themselves?

If you have hesitated about using local therapy or counseling over financial concerns, then a few quick online searches can put you in touch with state- and county-sponsored local programs or university-sponsored programs for very little cost. A lack of money should not stop any parent from seeking and locating affordable mental-health services. They are out there. Check your local yellow pages or online directory for Mental Health Services. Your local United Way should also offer resources.

2. **Placement with a Friend or Relative.** Is there a friend, relative, or mentor who would be willing to take your child in to remove her from her current negative environment? Before sending

Ashlyn to Carolina Springs, I had exhausted local therapy and had Ashlyn live with my mother, which lasted only ten days. But, in the end, I felt that at least I had exhausted this option before sending Ashlyn to residential treatment.

3. **Transferring Your Child to a Different School.** Have you tried to change your child's school? Investigating charter schools, reassigning your public school, or interviewing private or parochial schools and magnet programs may make a difference.

4. **Church Groups.** If a faith-centered environment is paramount to your concern for your child, look for church-affiliated or -sponsored programs for troubled teens.

5. **Local Parent Support Groups.** In some areas, your community may offer a parent support group that may provide a helpful exchange of empathy and advice. Ask your therapist, family doctor, chamber of commerce, library, local police station, or school guidance counselors for suggestions.

6. **Parent and Teen Coaching.** For years, we've been
hearing about adults who hire life coaches to
help motivate them to bring about positive
changes in their lives, both professionally and
personally. The benefits of working to one's
highest potential with this type of guidance are
clear. In light of this success, Parent and Teen
Coaching is becoming a growing trend.

Some parents will try working with a Certified
Parent Coach prior to making the decision to
send their child to residential therapy. This
approach allows the teen to live at home with the
parents. As with choosing a program for your
child's needs, finding the right coach for your
family may take some time and research. A Parent Coach can offer you objective views, ideas,
and most important, empower you to take control of a teenager who may be in the beginning
stages of spiraling out of control. If, however,
your child has reached a level of belligerence,
defiance, and outright self-destruction, this
coaching option may not be for you.

An Internet search for "Parent, Teen, Family,

or Life Coaches" or any variation of those key-
words will give you several sites to choose from.
Visit various websites and read about the services offered to learn more about this approach to
dealing with your teen. An Internet search
should also be able to help you locate coaches in
your area.

What *Not* to Do

As I already mentioned in Section One, avoid trying
to use military schools or ordinary boarding schools to
help you. These places are not set up for unwilling students, despite the sometimes stiff daily discipline they
may employ. Another option you may come across
during your search for proper facilities for your child's
needs is **Wilderness Programs**. Wilderness Programs, as
P.U.R.E. defines them, are run with a good deal of outdoor work and recreation, with only the most basic life
comforts. Wilderness Programs, in my opinion, are
short-term alternatives with short-term results. I've had
the opportunity to speak with parents who utilized
Wilderness Programs and realized that what they offered

their child was simply a good starting point. The short-term effectiveness of Wilderness Programs is rarely enough time for lasting rehabilitation and lasting results. Because of the extravagant cost of Wilderness Programs coupled with the high probability that the child will require further treatment, I usually advise parents to skip this step completely and choose a Residential Therapy program that provides the consistency a child requires in order to heal and grow emotionally. This is an example of why, as I mentioned earlier in the book, I am not convinced hiring an Educational Consultant is the answer. I have spoken with many families who, after hiring an Educational Consultant, were all referred to Wilderness Programs prior to any Residential Therapy. It can turn into an extra step that may be an unnecessary and expensive one.

Wilderness Programs are decidedly not **Boot Camps**, which are extreme places that I do not recommend, no matter how troubled a teenager may be. I believe the important difference between a Wilderness Program and a Boot Camp program is that Boot Camps, no matter what they call themselves or how they present their program, have *punishment* at the heart of their philosophy. The students are in such places to be punished, like you would expect to see in an old-time reform school. Hence the rough environments, intended as a constant message of deprivation. When in residence, children are usually forced to conform to harsh and punitive daily regimens, and they are further punished if they fail.

What truly fails is logic itself when we assume that angry and hostile teenagers can possibly improve in disposition by being thrust into a deliberately miserable situation where they are prodded to anger many times a day—and then consistently dared to react. At best, you will create a repressed kid who eventually leaves the program as a ticking bomb. Repression certainly works, in the short term, as every drill sergeant can affirm. But even a little bit of ordinary human insight casts doubt on any thought that teens can learn essential self-control or acquire a positive set of habits as a result of suffering prolonged deprivation, constant provocation, and a long list of potential infractions for which they are punished with bouts of isolation and short rations.

At first, many parents believe a Boot Camp would be the best choice for their child, as I did. It's easy to fall into a trap of making decisions using emotion, instead of logic. I wanted so badly for Ashlyn to see how good she had it, so sending her to a Boot Camp felt like a natural juxtaposition to her daily life to help her see that she should appreciate how fortunate she was. However, once that anger passed, I realized that what my child needed was quite the opposite, and I urge you to consider this, too.

Residential Therapy Programs

Say that you have gone through the alternatives explained at the beginning of this chapter, but found nothing that works for your particular situation. That is the point where all that remains is to select the Residential Therapy program that fits your needs.

Residential Therapy programs may be run as indoor operations, and set up more like traditional boarding schools, except for the added elements of discipline, security, and therapy. Your home location, relative to that of the program, should not factor into the program you choose. Avoid falling into the trap of using proximity as a criterion for "the best fit"; the program must be the best fit for your child's needs, even if that means the

added cost of a plane ride. This is a very expensive invest-
ment in your child's life, so you might as well choose the
best program—not proximity—for your child.

What should absolutely factor into the criterion for
the best fit is a program that encourages family partici-
pation. I tell parents on a daily basis that you cannot
have a program isolate you from your child. It is so
important to keep all lines of communication open. In
my experience, not being able to speak with my daughter for six months almost destroyed both of us. I cannot
begin to share the pain and emotional agony we went
through, but I was "trusting the program," as I was told
to do. However, many programs will ask parents not to
speak with the teen on the phone for the first 21–30 days
(not weeks or months), and this is completely reasonable, since these are the days in which the child experiences the most anger and the parent experiences the
most guilt. You should, however, be able to speak with
the therapist, director, owner, or assigned representative
at any time you wish during these first 21–30 days. Do
not allow the school to keep your child from you. It is
normal for a 21–30-day period of no contact. It is
normal to have your first visit at the three-month mark.

It is a red flag, however, if the program calls for deviating from these parameters.

You can simplify the dizzying list of names for the schools and their programs by realizing that each one will fall into one of two categories: a **Therapeutic Boarding School** (T.B.S.) or a **Residential Treatment Center** (R.T.C.). Both of these categories provide residential, structured programs for troubled teenagers. The choice between them essentially boils down to a program's degree of intensity:

1. **Therapeutic Boarding School** (T.B.S.). This place is set up to provide an environment for positive emotional growth, with an emphasis on behavior modification. The goal is pursued by a carefully designed and regulated daily life for each student. The program's overall structure mixes the practice of life skills with academics and therapy. The therapeutic aspect of a T.B.S., however, is not as intense as that of a Residential Treatment Center. At a Therapeutic Boarding School, a child may only expect to participate in one-on-one therapy sessions as infrequently as once a week, or even

biweekly. Group therapy is usually held every day, but positive social skills can also come from the atmosphere itself. There may be a licensed therapist on staff, but not necessarily on site. Young people can be transported to the therapist for examinations or scheduled sessions, as needed.

A T.B.S. uses what I call an all-encompassing approach. It is a comprehensive program that integrates all aspects of emotional, spiritual, and physical well-being. Their working philosophy is that a well-structured, positive, respectful, and disciplined living experience that is conducted over months at a time will be absorbed by the child as a natural process. Because we are all creatures with a survival instinct, every human being can be counted on to move toward experiences that are rewarding and move away from those that are not. The enforced discipline at a T.B.S. keeps the child in a position to directly control how satisfactory his experience is in that place. Approval, comfort, the respect of others, and the respect of oneself combine to forge powerful changes.

2. **Residential Treatment Center** (R.T.C.). An R.T.C.

is a much more clinical environment than a
Therapeutic Boarding School. You can expect an
on-site medical and psychological staff, with a
qualified medical staff member available 24/7.
This facility can be expected to provide the same
services that a Therapeutic Boarding School
offers, but with a more formal psychological
treatment. This is the sort of place where a parent
must turn when the child's behavior is so out of
control that it has become toxic and potentially
lethal.

An R.T.C. can attend to more serious psychological issues or behavior, including eating disor-
ders, self-mutilation, alcohol bingeing, drug
addiction, hypersexuality, and even small levels
of violence. However, dangerous teens who display
criminal behavior will still have to face the public
justice system if they cross the line and give in to
serious violence while they are there.

The Residential Treatment Center offers a
full-time, closed environment that specializes in
treatment and rehabilitation for young people
with chronic impairment issues or chemical

dependencies. An R.T.C. also provides on-site mental-health services for persons with a range of dysfunctions. The primary concern of every Residential Treatment Center, however, is therapeutic. All of the other services they may provide are really just in support of the ongoing task, which is to get at the source of a child's dysfunctional behavior and train her to work around it and through it.

Both a T.B.S. and R.T.C. will incorporate academics into daily life as well as work on life skills, and many offer accredited classroom work designed to allow teenagers to keep up with their academics. There is a fine line between a T.B.S. and R.T.C. As long as you've done your home-work, neither option can be wrong for your child. While investigating various programs, look for one that offers an interest that your child might have. Many programs are either centered around or include many of the following interests: culinary, computers, veterinary, equestrian, fine arts, music, horticulture, ranching, and sports, including skiing, snowboarding, tennis, etc. If you have not decided whether to utilize a T.B.S. or R.T.C., look for programs that offer activities that would appeal personally to your child.

Paying for Treatment

We have not discussed finances in great detail, but it can be safely assumed that most households do not have access to the ready cash necessary to pay these sorts of unforeseen bills. The costs are nothing that any person can shrug off. Families that can afford these costs, or those that are well-covered by their health-insurance plans, can indulge in the relative luxury of forging ahead with these difficult choices without having to fight the impacts of both the initial high costs and the ongoing drain of added fees. All others must be creative. Thus, an avalanche of financial books is available to help ordinary working people find access to cash, equity, and credit. These hard and cold financial realities exert a different impact upon every family, according to their means.

Those who find themselves unable to pay the considerable costs associated with treatment still have options. Your first is to ask the school you are interested in if they offer educational loans, similar to college loans. Ask your admissions director for a list of lenders that offer educational loans for their program. These loans are usually offered at a lower interest rate, have no prepayment penalties, and usually require no application fees. Further, a thorough Internet search combined with queries that you make of your own acquaintances, can steer you to grants, scholarships, and assistance programs for people in positions that match yours.

You can go the secular route with your search and seek out government-sponsored grants and loans at the county, state, and national level. In addition, if you are a person of religious faith, pursue assistance from that faith's formal organizations. Their programs were conceived and built by people who wanted to find ways to reach out to someone who is in a position like the one you find yourself in today. They understand that you do not want to ask for this help, but that your love for your child drives you to seek any source that may be available. And because they understand that about you and your family's situation, they will realize that you are in a battle to save one young person's life. I urge you not to be too proud to ask for financial help such as this, or from any other (legitimate) source that you can find.

Here is a real hot-button issue: Some parents have been known to use the child's college fund to pay for the program. I've seen people react in shock when I mention that fact in conversation. However, the justification for spending that college fund right now is compelling. If your teen stays on his destructive path, the question of college will likely be moot. What sort of success would your child have there? None of us must ever forget that by giving our teen an opportunity for a second chance at life, we are enhancing his or her chance of being able to *earn* their way through college later on. The goal is for you to be proud of your child at both graduations.

What You Can Expect to Pay

In nearly every instance, you must expect a Residential Treatment Center to have a base cost that approaches almost twice that of the Therapeutic Boarding School. For example, within the recent past, I have personally visited a Therapeutic Boarding School on the East Coast with a basic cost of $4,500 a month. The fee seemed fair for the program, by general comparison. It was right around that same time when I visited a Residential Treatment Center with a monthly fee of $8,900. That cost, too, is within the expected range for the program. With this in mind, a T.B.S. average length of stay is 9–12 months while an average length of stay for an R.T.C. is six months. What causes the cost discrepancy? It is the extra materials, staff hours, and staff expertise necessary to run an R.T.C. that is specifically designed to house out-of-control teenagers who may have deep substance-abuse issues. On-site medical and psychological staff are necessary to run an R.T.C. because the intensified therapeutic work done there requires that level of expertise. The medical officer on-site must be at least a qualified nurse or Emergency Medical Technician qualified to render any form of first aid and to direct the handoff to outside medical help, if the need arises. Typically, at least one psychologist (or some doctorate level of staff) or psychiatrist must be on-site, overseeing a staff of trained counselors who administer the day-to-day therapy for each child.

A Therapeutic Boarding School can be expected to cost less because it has fewer financial demands to serve. And while the lower cost of a T.B.S. is still enough to blow away your savings or put you into bankruptcy, any child in their program *who will embrace it* can literally construct a new life pattern for themselves. Inside the program, enrollees will acquire an entire range of social behaviors that they had not, for whatever reason, absorbed in the past. That newly acquired palette of effective social responses will give them a form of social power that they will be able to feel for themselves, long before they go back home, while they practice it in skillfully guided group sessions.

Here's what your bone-crushing fees pay for:

- **Reinforced physical security** around the location. All of the grounds are set up to direct and control the movements of young people who most likely do not want to be there. Many would escape if given the chance.

- **Security staff** will naturally be required to handle a population of belligerent young people who consider themselves prisoners. And because of the increased likelihood of physical or verbal confrontations with the most troubled kids, this also raises the level of training and expertise required of an effective staff member.

- **Medical and psychological staff members.**
  Whether an R.T.C. requires 24/7 on-site
  professionals or a T.B.S. has access to highly
  skilled professionals, these professionals still
  need to get paid.

- **General overhead costs,** including food, lodging,
  program materials, maintenance of grounds,
  sporting facilities, laundry facilities, etc., are,
  of course, also funded by your tuition.

And that's the way the money goes.

Remember: Residential Therapy represents a child's
last stop before landing in society's underbelly. After that,
there is no place left for a troubled teen to go, except the
criminal justice system, a state hospital, or the streets.
You will find that all of the *good* Residential Therapy
programs make that grim fact a part of their operating
mission. They take their last-ditch position just as seriously as you do. They know that if their program fails to
reach your child, then that young person's life journey
will soon turn very dark indeed.

6

Transporting Your Teen to the Program Site

Everyone who knows me knows that I prefer to deal in plain talk, and that I don't like to dance around when handling testy issues. I won't shy away from plain talk now, either. So let's just say it—this is "the killer chapter" of the book.

It delves into both the myths and the realities of that terrible question lurking in the back (or maybe even hanging out in the front) of the mind of every parent: **What if my child reeeally objects to going?**

Are you afraid to let your teenager know about your plans for fear that she will run off and disappear, thereby taking away your opportunity for intervention? These are dreadful things for any parent to consider, but every aspect of this process boils down to the issue of getting the teen to the location and into the program. No matter how carefully we choose the place for our child, we still have to get him or her there.

It's wonderful if you have a child you can speak to about such things, and who is willing to give it a try. But the colder reality is this: if your child really is that mature and self-restrained, then the extreme choice of Residential Therapy might be avoided in the first place. Once in a while, I meet a parent who is fortunate enough to have this kind of situation with their child, who can explain things to their child in such a way that the child voluntarily comes along and enrolls without difficulty.

But, of course, most teens whose behavior has forced the parent(s) to consider this process in the first place are not inclined to cooperate with adult authority about much of anything. The darker challenge that these kids represent gives parents everywhere the willies.

These parents know that the "same old stuff" is not

working with their kid anymore, and they know that real action is needed. But, on the other hand, they may fear calling up a twenty-first-century version of "the boys in white coats," and dragging their child off to an asylum. They wonder how any child could ever recover from the sense of betrayal that must be suffered during the trauma of being captured, kidnapped, and committed.

Honestly, the unwilling child is certain to experience a strong sense of betrayal and an equally strong flash of anger. But, and this is important, your child *can* recover from that understandable sense of betrayal. He will do so to the degree that his sense of personal responsibility is stimulated *by the program.*

This is a reasonable expectation for you, as the parent(s) making the tough choices and sticking with the unpleasant issues. It is reasonable because you are set on fixing this problem, and on doing it as best you can. A working premise of *any* effective teen-help program is: **Every individual has the capacity to understand what their own behavior has forced others to do *in response to them.***

In the right program, this point of personal maturity is required of everyone and will prove to be essential to your child's individual progress. And so, no matter what means you have to employ to guarantee that your child (1) safely arrives at the program site; and (2) gets properly enrolled, his own sense of responsibility and social accountability will tell him to forgive you for any actions that *he forced you to take*. It is not likely to come on that first day, or even in the first weeks. It may not arrive for a long while. It will be well worth the wait, however, when it comes. For the time being, you as the adult in the equation must apply your patience to this extraordinary situation in the same way that you would apply a bandage to a wound. This is one of those points in the life of a functional adult when it no longer matters how anything "feels" to us. We grit our teeth and get the job done.

Give the healing process time to work. It is up to the teenager to deal with her sense of trauma, a task that she alone will have to carry out. However, respecting the need for events to play out in their proper time—whether or not that time frame is personally convenient—is a task that none of us can afford to avoid.

Pride may keep a child from wanting to admit it, for a while, but the indelible sign of emerging maturity will be his ability to step back from his own emotions enough to realize that you have acted on his best behalf. And it is just this sort of emerging maturity that you can turn to Residential Therapy programs to achieve.

No matter how one program may differ from the other in appearance and style, the underlying value shared by the best programs must be to strengthen the child's sense of personal responsibility and personal accountability. In kids where such things appear to be entirely missing, then fundamental systems of personal responsibility and social accountability will be built from scratch. It will be done by example. It will be uniformly applied. It will be enforced with the threat of lost privileges, and cooperation will be rewarded with expanded opportunities.

The primary means of achieving this is to base the child's complete experience of his daily environment on *the results of his own behavior*. There will be a strong system of earned privileges, in an environment where a key part of the strategy is to begin with allowing a child virtually none at all. In this way, even small things become valuable and are therefore capable of motivating a child's cooperation. This type of controlled environment ensures that the program is given the time and opportunity to actually work for each child.

Breaking the News

If your child is not prone to violent behavior, but would still be at risk as a runaway if you tried to plan out the move with her, then you may elect to use deception as a passive means of transporting her to the program site. In that case, you simply base the nature of the story that you tell her on whatever you think might motivate her to get in the car and take a trip with you. As I mentioned previously, not telling the child is a frequent choice parents make to ensure their child will not run away before they have a chance to get her into the program.

The child will be furious with you once she realizes what has happened. But by then, the staff members will be there to ensure order. The enrollment process will go forward with or without her overt cooperation. In worst-case scenarios, the enforced enrollment process will be something like being booked into jail. There is an official process that is carried out as politely as the child allows it to be—but that will be carried out, nonetheless.

Perhaps the toughest aspect of "the killer chapter" is the one that addresses some people's personal images of Residential Therapy for teens. We all know the kind of images I'm referring to: terrified kids being dragged away to a de facto reform school, screaming for help, perhaps screaming for revenge.

Any lingering doubts that you may have about this process will be triggered with these thoughts. Now is the time to work through them, if you are going to be able to work through them at all. Guilt is a monster that attacks all of us in such an emotionally charged process. Give yourself time to fight it off. You do that through satisfying your doubts by insisting on obtaining clear and accurate information from the program representatives regarding every aspect of your child's life in their facility. You need to know what your child's daily life will be like if you commit to placing him or her under the care of these people and their program. (See Chapter 7, Evaluating Residential Therapy Programs.)

An Alternative to Deception

If you loathe the idea of telling a false story to get your kid into the car, but you still dread some sort of terrible emotional scene and a potential explosion, then that leads you to the consideration of using an **Expert Transportation Service.**

For such a delicate task, we can all acknowledge that an ordinary taxicab or airport limousine is not going to cut it. The specific kind of transport service I am referring to here is the use of *trained* drivers and escorts to safely remove the teen from the home and see him through to his safe arrival at the facility. These transport services are desirable when you have a child who may act out in hysteria. Without the protection and assurance that such a service provides, the risks of injury to any or all of the parties involved are just too much for any responsible person to assume.

Ask the school for a list of recommended escort services that you can contact and interview to determine which one you desire to work with. Many parents interview at least two services to compare rates, availability, and procedure. Once you have hired your preferred service, you will be provided with specific instructions regarding their arrival at your home. It is common and normal for a service to arrive at a very early hour in the morning, sometimes even before dawn. There are several good reasons for this: the child is usually home; the child is usually asleep and off guard; an early start increases the probability that a child will sleep through the trip; and, it enables your child to arrive during daylight hours.

Many of these transportation experts have a degree in Behavioral Science and are familiar with dealing with kids in such difficult circumstances. It is imperative that you ask the transport company whether they are licensed and insured to transport teens. The *safety* of your child should be your primary concern. This priority will also be communicated to the child by the way in which this whole transportation experience is carried out. It's true that the harder they fight, the more it will feel like an arrest to them. However, they will quickly see that the more they cooperate, the more the entire experience will relax into a far more tolerable one for them.

This is why the moment that the transport car pulls up in front of your home, the message of *firm but fair* is communicated to your teenager in the form of action, as much as in words. Ask your transport people what procedure they take in regard to speaking with your child about this process. We all know that teenagers have ears approximately ten thousand times more sensitive to b.s. than normal human beings. They register how adults behave far more strongly than by anything those adults might choose to say. In a good therapeutic program and transport service, *firm but fair* is communicated on as many levels as possible, all of the time.

This is why your recovering child will ultimately accept and embrace your difficult choice, along with the sacrifice of time, money, and emotional concern that you will employ to throw them this lifeline. At the end, the whole experience will have been about growing up for them. That is the heart of it. Any residual anger or resentment that they may hold for you and for others will eventually be overridden by their developing understanding of their own role in having made that lifeline necessary.

7

Evaluating Residential Therapy Programs

Once you have personalized your list of potential programs based upon (a) location; (b) style of program; and (c) price, you will arrive at the point of interviewing a representative for each one. Now, you must be prepared to keep your cool while you also retain your focus, and then politely but firmly ask for *specific answers* to these fifteen key questions:

1. Can I speak with the program's owner, director, or therapist? Avoid desperate salespeople, who may be tempted to advise you based upon a commission. You must politely but firmly ask to speak *only* to the program owner, director, or therapist.

Yes, it's true that all of these people hold important positions. They will always have many other pressing matters to attend to besides taking the time to talk with you. And yes, their time is valuable.

Your child isn't?

The people you trust with your child's life must be the ones who have all of the important sources of information at hand, including the school's academic accreditations, how they are licensed, background of the staff, school philosophy and mission statement, the effectiveness of their program, how the actual program works, i.e., the program model and specifically how it can work for your child. It is important to review the parent/student handbook before making a commitment to the school to ensure you are comfortable with the logistics of their program.

Speaking to a person in a position of authority at the school is critical because he or she is at the level where there is a *vested interest in the program*. They only want kids whom they believe they can help. They are far less tempted than a sales rep would be to simply sweep your child into their program because of a desire to get a commission. After all, they know that an incorrigible kid drains the program of staff time and energy, resources that are ultimately wasted on an unreachable teenager, but which are stolen, meanwhile, from the others. They clearly appreciate that this loss of staff energy threatens their bottom line.

Here's how you can tell the difference between a sales representative and a responsible manager and/or admissions director. Since a reputable program and person are interested in determining whether your child is going to present an unmanageable challenge to their program, they will be more willing to take the time to converse with you than a sales rep would be. Even though they are taking time to speak with you for their own purposes, you can make that fact work for you by taking the opportunity to get complete answers to all of your concerns, and by keeping at it until you feel satisfied.

If the art of remaining calm but also remaining focused and determined while you speak is difficult for you, then please reassure yourself with the knowledge that you are not responsible for whether they feel irritated by your persistent questions. You are responsible for a family member who probably does not know it, but needs your immediate and direct intervention as their last and best lifeline.

2. Does the program provide a parent reference list? If your program representative is able to give you assurances that make you feel comfortable about its suitability for your child, you will probably be provided with a reference list of parents who have or who have had children in the program. It is always beneficial to speak with them, but remember that since the school gave them to you, they're most likely to be positive references. If you want to hear from parents who are not on the parent reference list, which can sometimes give you more objective feedback, you can call listed parents and ask them for another parent to call. As a parent who had a child in a program, I always knew other parents with kids in the same program, so getting the name and number of a parent not on the reference list shouldn't be a problem.

Ask each parent how long his or her child was in the program. Look for a general average. This little detective game takes patience, but these may be some of the most important questions that you ask in this whole process. Remember, you are searching for impartial information to help you make a life-changing decision on behalf of your troubled child. It may be life changing for you, as well. So it is only by embracing the necessary detective work at this point that you can significantly raise the chance that those life changes will be for the better. There is no reason to be shy about it. *You have the right to know.*

An excellent question to ask all reference parents is: *If you could change one thing about the program, what would it be?* This can be very telling and also bring out some of the negatives. Remember, there are no perfect programs, but if you go in with your eyes wide open, chances are you will be ready for anything. I believe that, as parents, we need to weigh the negatives versus the positives. If a reference parent complains that there wasn't enough therapy, you may want to ask the program director about the therapy schedule and how it is monitored. Keep in mind that all students are different and have unique needs, so if one student requires more than another, it may be a complaint that you don't need to be concerned with.

3. Is the program state-licensed and accredited academically as a school? This is a simple one. Both answers should be yes. Ask to see a copy of their license and accreditations. Check the date to confirm that the license is still valid. If you have questions regarding the license, contact the State Department of Licensing to confirm that the program is truly in good standing.

4. What are the program director's credentials? Review the director's educational background (the level of degrees he or she holds), as well as how long the director has been employed by the school and his or her experience in the teen-help industry as a whole. Also verify:

(a) How are the staff members *trained* and *certified*? Are staff members certified to physically handle a child without harming him? Is the staff certified in CPR? Are staff members familiar with the school's fire policy and emergency plans? Does the school require its staff to fulfill continuing education through seminars, conferences, classes, etc.?

(b) Are the teachers and therapists *licensed* in their professions? Inquire about the educational backgrounds of the teachers and therapists. Do they meet your needs? For instance, some therapists will be Licensed Clinical Social Workers (LCSW), psychologists, or psychiatrists. Knowing the therapists' backgrounds can help you determine the best fit for your child's needs. Depending on the situation, some parents would prefer a psychologist instead of a LCSW or vice versa, so it's important to be clear on what to expect once your child is enrolled. If your child has special educational needs, be sure they are covered in these credentials. For example, if your child has a learning disability, it is important to know they have a teacher available who can work with your specific requirements.

(c) Does the program run *background checks* on staff members prior to employment? Child predators typically seek out jobs that allow them greater access to children, so this is imperative to know.

I know that many people find it difficult to question
someone in authority, and they fear coming off as
being confrontational. However, these people are
supposed to already know and appreciate the fact that
you are in the midst of making a terribly difficult and
important decision, and that you must have as much
information as possible. I believe that if they make a
show out of being "too busy" to deal with your
questions, then that should be considered a giant red
flag. Their essential failure to understand and address
your position would call into question that quality of
judgment that you must count on them to employ
24/7 on behalf of your teen.

Anything less should get a big thumbs-down
from you.

5. Will I be able to speak with my child? How often?
And similarly:

(a) Can I visit my child in person? By video
conference? And *when*?

(b) Will my child's postal mail be monitored or
censored, going out *or* coming in? If so, why?

These questions must be answered to your satisfaction. Don't settle for glittering generalities, such as telling you that the child will be allowed to communicate once they "reach" a given level or position. If they say that, you should realize that it is then easy for the program to use that restriction to manipulate the child's ability to communicate with home at all. In most schools and programs, we find that the answer you should shoot for is that they want about three weeks before you have your first phone conversation with your child. This "time-out" period serves the purpose of giving your child time to adapt to the place without outside support or distraction. (They do *not* need calls from home telling them how tough this whole thing is on you.)

We find that personal visitation is generally permitted sometime within the three-month mark, and I do not recommend that any child should be allowed to go any longer than that without a visit, unless there is some unique situation that you have been advised about and with which you agree. My concern will always be that no matter what the rationale there may be for any greater delay in communication, there could be serious abandonment issues on the child's part if that time period is drawn out too far.

As for allowing the child to communicate with friends and relatives, we find that the usual practice is for the school to restrict electronic communication devices altogether, as well as landline telephones or faxes, and to send all of the child's outgoing postal mail to the parent(s). You can then sort it and determine if it should go out to friends and family or not.

I firmly believe that parents should elect to read all of the mail, *no matter who it is addressed to*, especially if they have any reason to suspect that arrangements are being made for the delivery of contraband or for an assisted escape. Personal privacy, after all, is not a "right" for a minor child—it is a privilege. Your child is not in the position to receive that privilege for the time being.

The school representative should be willing to assure you that they will not hold back any of the child's postal mail to you for any reason whatsoever. You must not allow them to use your own communication line with your child as a bargaining chip with the child once he or she is inside. No matter what argument may be presented to you, your communication with the child (and theirs with you, on some reasonable basis) is not on the negotiating table. As parents, we not only have the right to know what is going on but we have the obligation.

6. What types of financing are offered? Are there scholarships? Also ask:

   (a) Are there any *extra fees* that are not included in tuition? Specifically, what are those *extra fees,* and when must they be paid?

   (b) Will my personal insurance cover any of these costs?

Most families who cannot afford fees ranging up to $400 *per day* for up to two years will rely on formal or informal loans to pay off these programs. Informal loans through a rich uncle are great, if you have one. For those of us who picked our ancestors poorly, we will have to go the route of the formal bank loan or home equity loan.

If the program you have in mind has licensed doctors or therapists on staff, or is a member of the Joint Commission association of the healthcare organization, your medical insurance may pick up a significant portion of the cost. Either way, the financial pain that is associated with this process is real. Despair and anger are understandable problems for whomever has to ultimately pick up the check. This is a time of stress and great challenge for everyone involved.

Ask the program's *qualified* representative for the names of any lenders that the program has on file. These lending institutions may have certain loan programs with special, low-interest rates or with easier payback terms. Remember, they are motivated to accommodate you.

Be sure to ask if the child's *therapy visits* are included in the basic cost of the program, and if they are not, what are the "add-ons"? Check the same thing about their *educational expenses*. Press them again about any financial add-ons at this point.

If you do take the formal loan route, ask your lender if there are interest breaks for the program's purpose. You may also find that the mental healthcare aspect of the program is tax-deductible.

Does your child have an Individual Education Plan (IEP) through the school district? It may help you to defer some of the expenses in the academic component of the program. If you have an IEP in place for your child, it is important to ask the program representative if they will work with an IEP, and to discuss the reimbursement process with them.

7. What is the average length of stay for the students? And similarly:

(a) Do they offer an *aftercare program* or a *transitional program*? Is there a fee for aftercare?

(b) Can my child go back to the program for a second time if he is struggling again?

As mentioned previously, the length of time ranges from about six months at a minimum to as much as two years in more extreme cases. An average length of stay will be within *nine to twelve months.*

When speaking with other parents, ask how long their child was in the program before their successful completion. While we must never forget that all families will have their unique sets of problems and challenges, you should be able to detect the average range of stay to expect for your child just by asking several other parents how long their child was in, or how long they are projected to be there.

Aftercare is such an important issue that you should make it one of your most persuasive deciding factors. Be sure that they clearly explain to you whether they offer any services for a child after graduation and if there are any additional costs for that service. You need to know whether or not this program has a system in place to help the family to make the transition back to living under one roof again. Ask if you can continue any sort of family counseling through the program, perhaps even by phone or Internet conference.

Some programs allow a child to return, if necessary, after making the transition out. Some do not. You need to know whether your child can return to the place, if for any reason they begin to backslide into their destructive patterns of behavior. Don't try to predict whether or not your child will need that service; just be certain to verify that the service is available in a form that your family can utilize. Return visits are sometimes offered at *no* cost—if the child completes the program before leaving.

Since the rough patches of daily life are inevitable

for everyone, your teen's reaction to them after the return home will be your most powerful indicator of their degree of success with the program. This is not to say that they must not show signs of anger or frustration; it means that they should be able to display a consistent familiarity with the basic emotional coping skills that must be present for anyone to enjoy long-term success on the outside. More than anything else, a parent hopes for a program that will be able to instill a fundamental set of coping skills that will manifest in the child's behavior.

However, each child differs in his reaction to Residential Therapy, and each one takes his own version of the program home with him. Even the best programs can never be regarded as a fix-all. There will always be slips. The real sign of actual progress for your teen and your family will be seen in the way that child recovers or fails to recover from slips. For example, if your child is caught smoking pot after coming back home and rejoining the family, all of my experience has shown me that it is that child's *own* reaction to having picked up the joint that really matters. Do they see it as "proof" that the program did not work for them, and therefore an open excuse to return to old negative behaviors? Or can they see it as an isolated "slip" in an otherwise good plan, one they still want to live out from day to day? That difference in attitude is crucial to their chance for recovery.

You will know that the program has shown its value if your child is able to take a long-term view of their short-term slip and chooses to react to it by strengthening their resolve, instead of abandoning it.

That level of *personal choice* is the "X" factor in post-program life. It is also why we struggle to come up with accurate "success rates" for any given program. You can really only judge the way that the program itself is carried out after time has passed. The final word as to its success will not come until months down the road, perhaps even years, when each individual has had the chance to make the program's training manifest in their lives. All of us who have been there know—and any family with a child in the program will soon discover—that "success" is nothing more or less than what the child, the parent, and the family make of the Residential Therapy experience. While your child is the focus of this struggle, any lasting success that comes out of it will be a team effort.

8. What is the average student age in the program?
Also ask:

(a) What is the *population capacity* of the program,
in terms of how many students the program is
licensed to accommodate, and how many are
currently enrolled there?

(b) What is the *student-to-staff ratio*?

It is so important that your child be placed in
the appropriate element, both in terms of age and
gender, and also in terms of not being lumped in with
dangerous others. This is one of the reasons that
staff-student ratios are so vital. If the staff is too
heavily outnumbered, then it will not matter if they are
well trained and dedicated in their work. They will be
overwhelmed by the workload, and your child will not
only suffer the neglect, but be in harm's way if left
unguarded among kids who may be prone to violence.

At P.U.R.E., we have found the ideal student-staff
ratio to be between one-to-four and one-to-seven. This
range has shown itself to be reasonable, and if the staff
is well-trained and supervised, it is a sufficient ratio to

maintain order and administer the daily program.

These particular questions will be tailored by you, according to your own needs and preferences. Some parents want a large program so that their child gets a range of social experience. Some want a small place where they feel the child will get more individual attention. You may want a co-ed environment, or prefer a single-gender experience for your child, especially if heterosexual hypersexuality has been a problem.

If you prefer a co-ed environment, ask them how they keep the kids separated, especially the sleeping accommodations.

9. Does the program offer open enrollment?

This is a vital service. When your child is in crisis, you want to be able to deliver the child immediately. A school that offers enrollment at set times or by semester or around holidays is not a school for troubled teens. Aside from the program's weekend status, some will only offer enrollment at certain scheduled times of the year. You will generally find that traditional boarding schools and military schools tend to have enrollment periods limited to the structure of their school term.

By contrast, I have found that most programs that are geared toward troubled teens will offer open enrollment. They acknowledge that dysfunctional behavior does not change according to the month or season.

10. Where is the nearest medical facility and/or full hospital? And similarly:

(a) Does the program have a *physician* or *registered nurse* on staff and on premises?

(b) Does the program accept kids on medication? If your child is on prescribed medication, who will dispense it and how will it be monitored? Is there a system in place to monitor the safety and effectiveness of the prescribed medication?

(c) Does the school meet your child's specific medical needs? For instance, if your child is insulin-dependent, physically challenged, has asthma, or a severe food allergy, is the school equipped to administer proper care for these conditions?

11. Are they academically accredited? Will the child's school credits transfer back home? Also find out, if applicable:

(a) Do they offer S.A.T. and A.C.T. testing?

(b) Do they offer special educational help?

(c) As icing on the cake, do they offer any form of extracurricular activities? Are there extra fees for special tutoring and/or extracurricular activities?

(d) Do they offer college courses or vocational training for older students?

Before signing over your child to their care, get a copy of both their *accreditation* and their *school program*. Do not allow anyone to make you feel as if you are digging too deep when you check these things out. These questions are the only way to assure that the child's education will not be unduly sacrificed during their time in the Residential Therapy program. Just because you are willing to accept that some degree of slip must be reasonably allowed, given the circumstances, does not mean that educational concerns ever go out the window. This is always done with an eye for the day that the child returns home and must begin reintegration into daily life.

With those assurances in place, follow up with the child's regular school and verify, from their end, that the credits amassed by your child during their time in the program will indeed be accepted there when your child returns.

It is also important to know if the fundamentals of physical fitness are effectively addressed in the daily lives of kids through the program. In addition, are there team and individual sports available? Sporting teamwork can be a great way for kids to learn cooperation and to raise their own self-respect. The sports program should emphasize building up the child, physically and mentally, rather than focusing on the competitive ego-fest that sometimes describes sports programs at regular high schools. Screaming coaches and the pressure to win are not helpful components of life in a good Residential Therapy program.

12. Does the program accept involuntary enrollment? And similarly:

(a) Will they accept enrollment from kids who have

to be *professionally escorted* there to show up?
Does the program offer escort services? (For
further definitions and advice on escort services,
see Chapter 6.)

(b) Do they accept court-appointed teens and teens
with criminal records? You need to know this
whether that describes your child or not. It has to
do with the element that you can expect your
child to walk among during his or her time in the
program.

(c) What is their policy on expelling a child? You
should know that most teen-help programs are
not inclined to expel a child, since behavioral
problems are the reason that they are there in the
first place. Unless a child suffers a psychotic
break or resorts to overt violence, most programs
believe that the best answer is for the child to
spend more time there, not less.

Once again, you need to ask about this regardless of
the state of your child's behavior because it also tells
you about the environment that he or she will be in.

It runs contrary to logic to dump our troubled kids in with a pack of sociopaths for months or even years, and then expect them to come out with their emotional balance restored and a renewed determination to live a positive life. If the environment around them is not corrective, but simply restrictive and depressing, where are they supposed to acquire the missing ingredients for acceptable behavior, regard for others, and self-esteem?

13. Is the facility secured? Fenced? Also ask:

(a) How do they keep the kids from running off? Often, the main method of restraint is simply for the owners to locate the program out in the boondocks near some small town, so that there really is no place for an escapee to go. The possibility of a kid escaping with outside assistance ought to be highly remote, since communication is generally controlled by the program and the parent(s), which should prevent the necessary outside contact.

(b) When it comes to personal restraint, what methods does the program employ? Ask them what their policy is in dealing with a student who is completely lost in a rage, perhaps out of control and threatening himself or others. Here again, you should know this whether it applies to your child or not, as it reflects directly on the environment that they might inhabit. Many programs use the Mandt System (www. mandtsystem.com), which is a method of calming the child by holding them down until they are over the momentary danger of harm. If your program uses the Mandt System or another familiar system such as Crisis Prevention (www.crisisprevention.com), be certain that the staff is trained and certified, and that someone with such training and certification is *always present on the premises 24/7.*

(c) What is the program's policy about *consequences* if the students don't follow the rules? Most schools have time-out areas, but they should not be scary isolation rooms, and the program should *never* employ isolation boxes. Threatening the child's fundamental sense of personal safety is counter-productive. It is my belief and experience that doing so builds resentment, anger, and anxiety.

An example of a more reasonable way of handling misbehavior by a student, say for a runaway who is caught and brought back, is to make them dress in a brightly colored jumpsuit (usually orange) for a determined amount of time, using the sheer conspicuousness of the outfit as a consequence of social pressure. Ask them what *they* would do with such a child.

14. What about the physical place itself? What is the housing like?

In an ideal world, parents would be able to visit several schools/programs before making a decision. (See "Visiting the Facility" later in this chapter for advice on optimizing your visit to a facility.) But, realistically, whether due to time constraints or financial reasons, many parents simply cannot make the visits. If you fall into this category, don't feel guilty about it as long as you are doing your due diligence to research the school. By speaking with parents and possibly former students who have attended, you should get a good sense of where you are sending your child. Most programs welcome visits prior to placement. If they don't, I would definitely hesitate considering that school. Also ask:

(a) What type of food is served? Is it a health-oriented menu? In many cases, the food is more or less cafeteria-style, as in your local public school. It is very common for parents to ask for an example of the menu that is served to the children as well as what types of snacks they offer.

(b) Is there a school uniform or uniform code? If so, what is the cost?

As far as your evaluation of the physical location itself, whether you go in person or whether you check out photos and websites, the standard of concern is that while these programs are not designed to offer the amenities of home, they are not supposed to represent hell either. Even in so-called Boot Camps for troubled kids, the thing that makes them punitive and extreme is not the physical environment. It is the *atmosphere* created by the general level of hostility and fear that is afflicted upon the kids as part of that particular program's ongoing control methods. It is that atmosphere, most of all, that you must look out for when you evaluate any Residential Therapy program.

15. Do I have to sign a contract, also known as an enrollment agreement? In most cases, the answer is *yes*. Signing this contract is going to be extremely important and must be undertaken with the utmost concern and caution. Some key points to review:

- What is the duration of the contract?

- If you break the contract, what are the penalties?

- What exactly does the contract entail?

- If your child is expelled from the program, does the contract release you from financial obligation for the duration of the program?

- Does the contract outline the costs you are aware of and the services you have been told? Be sure that you are aware of the fees that can be charged to you. In other words, confirm that what you have been told is covered in the contract.

Since contracts are usually filled with legalese that the layman may not be familiar with, it is a good idea to have an attorney review the contract. If you have a relative or friend who is a lawyer, they may be able to help you. If not, it might be worth paying a lawyer to review the contract. As it shouldn't take that long, it should not be too costly, and it could help you to better understand what you are committing to. In my opinion, it would be a very worthwhile fee and could potentially save you thousands in the end.

Another clause that is in most contracts gives the program "temporary" custody of the child in the event that they need to have medical treatment urgently or if the child runs away and gets picked up by the local authorities. They will only release the child to a custodial parent or guardian. In most contracts, it will usually plainly state that this is no way supersedes or replaces the rights of the parent, which means they will always communicate with the parent and submit to the parent regarding decisions for their child.

Visiting the Facility

The process of visiting schools and programs is one of our most important jobs at P.U.R.E. The knowledge we gather lies at the heart of the work we do. For this reason, we can bring a real measure of assurance to concerned parents who have a child in crisis. Inspection is vital to determining if we can recommend any school or program. In addition to the work that I personally do, many of the reporters who keep me informed are parents who have had to deal with these issues themselves, which is why one of P.U.R.E.'s slogans is "Real Parents, Real Experiences." Therefore, with every report that we take in, it is as if we have been investigating a place for our own child.

If you find that it is possible for you to visit the program you have tentatively selected, you need to go at this task with a balanced and well-rounded list of concerns. The ones that follow are direct examples of the ways that I check out a school or program myself and are also the same categories that we double-check through our contributors.

1. Visit on a weekday. Experience confirms that it is always best to visit the program during the week, so that we can observe their daily routine during school hours. Most programs prefer that you make an appointment to visit them, and understandably so, to insure that key staff members are there to give you the full tour and so you can meet the director and

therapists. However, you should be able to stop in anytime (within reason) and without notice, but with the
risk that appropriate staff members will not be there or
unavailable. It is almost impossible to meet all the staff,
including weekend and night staff, but meeting with
the owner and/or director should be a priority on your
agenda.

2. Listen to your intuition. From the moment you arrive,
what does your intuition tell you? We each have an
innate "parent meter" that goes off and lets us know if
something doesn't feel right. Listen to it! I wish I had.
What are your first impressions about the general atmosphere of the place? How do you feel when you get out of
your car? Of course, there is apprehension, but is there a
sense of security, kindness, nurturing—or do you feel
cold and fearful? Usually from the moment I step onto a
campus, I can get a vibe, good or bad. In some cases, it is
not so good, but after the initial ice breaks, I realize the
beauty within. Remember, this is not easy and not natural, so be prepared for many emotions. But in the end, let
your head and heart combined make the decision. People
who make it a point to visit a number of these places

consistently confirm my own observation that there is a
dramatic difference in the general feeling from one place
to the next.

Take note if you sense a cold and unfriendly
atmosphere, and be sure to note the difference when
you walk into a program where the feel of the place
is warm and nurturing right from the beginning.
Assuming that the two places are equally competent at
handling their security issues, which place would you
want for your child? This is especially true if you agree
with my philosophy that *punishment* has no place.
This is a place designed to reconstruct dysfunctional
behavior while reinforcing a child's positive traits.

3. Assess the outside environment. What are the
grounds like? Are they groomed and well maintained?
Do they appear to be there just for looks, or do they
figure into the daily experience of the kids? For
example, some Residential Therapy programs take
advantage of an outdoor locale to set up a ropes
course. These treetop challenges require the use of balance and the control of instinctive fear. The kids also
get great exercise while they work their way across the

course. Naturally, you make a special point to ask about their safety procedures.

Do they have domestic, farm, or ranch animals on-site? Animal care is a grounding and stabilizing experience for anyone. You don't necessarily need to see livestock. Any domesticated animal will do because the maturing effect is imparted by the *process* of the daily care and feeding of any warm-blooded creature that is capable of individually recognizing and reacting to each person, based upon that person's behavior.

How well are the animals kept, in terms of their stables, pens, or kennels? The accommodations don't have to be anything fancy, but they do need to be secure from breakout, protected from potential abuse by any troubled child, and generally kept in a condition that reflects an appropriate sense of *personal responsibility* in caring for them.

4. Check out the living accommodations. At a Residential Therapy program, you should expect accommodations that meet your child's basic needs. It is not a vacation camp. Amusement is not the purpose. But neither is your child going off to prison. Therefore, the best tone that can be set by the place itself will bear out the message that this is a place where each individual will be cared for, but where the focus will always be upon the therapeutic work and emotional growth that is to be done.

If you spot any physical disrepair, ask yourself if it appears to be an issue of neglected upkeep, or from possible student-inflicted damages. For example, it is not uncommon to see a fist-sized hole or holes punched into a wall; you are looking at a housing place for kids who are often deeply angry and openly hostile. Even passive kids can be prone to sudden outbreaks of temper. Therefore, signs of recent damages are reasonable, to some extent, but any evidence of long-term neglect remains cause for suspicion.

Do you see or smell mold? That could be cause for concern. Ask about what you see or smell if you suspect this.

While many Residential Therapy programs are carried out in places that are very basic as far as having amenities, they must still meet reasonable human survival needs. Many such places are housed in remodeled older homes. Students may sleep in bunk beds, each with a set of drawers or small storage cabinet. The housing area will most likely have a living room or common room, a therapy room, and perhaps a computer room for those who prove themselves to be responsible in taking care of property. Other than meeting those essential requirements, the real effect of the program is not brought about by the physical environment, but by the dynamics of the program itself, as it is administered by *trained and monitored* staff members. I cannot emphasize this enough: Don't judge a book by its cover. A modest-looking environment is not an indication that the program is not equipped with the very best staff. Again, it's the program structure itself and the qualifications of the staff that matter most.

5. Evaluate the staff. I am always interested in the general demeanor of the staff members. In speaking with them, I listen to their overall tone of voice. Does it portray a controlled, professional person? Does it reflect energy and enthusiasm? Does it reveal boredom or sarcasm of any kind? A person's voice will often betray more truth than they intend to tell.

Visit the business office and review the credentials of

the school as well as the staff. This is your first real exposure to the professional basis of the facility, beyond any salesmanship or hype about the place that you may experience from people who know why you are there. *People with nothing to hide* will understand your concern about qualifications and credentials. As long as they are treated with respect, they have no valid reason to refuse you. I have never had a school deny P.U.R.E. the chance to review licenses and credentials. Personally, I have even been welcomed to take copies of the staff's certifications and licenses for P.U.R.E.'s file. After all, doctors and lawyers all put them right up on their walls, and the program's staff members are doing work that is no less important to the health and welfare of every one of the children there. Most programs are very happy to show you their staff's credentials. In the event your visit takes place during the week, this is also an opportune time to ask about the night and weekend staff and their qualifications.

6. Pay attention to the students. Another major impression that you gather about a residential program, after taking in the feel of the physical surroundings and reviewing staff credentials, will come directly from the students. It is a common practice for a program to have its upper-level students give you a guided tour. In some cases, the director will accompany you and give you the opportunity to have private time with the kids.

This part does not require a trained expert to make a sound judgment, just a concerned person who is willing to use his eyes and ears, ask questions, and respectfully listen.

For openers, how do the kids look, especially those who have been in the program for several months or more? Is their physical appearance robust? Do they radiate anger or hostility? When you address them, are they responsive, and if so, are they reasonably polite?

My experience when visiting Residential Therapy programs on behalf of P.U.R.E. is that the students are usually quite friendly, and as a result of their many group and individual sessions, they are often able to discuss the reasons they are there with a real degree of insight. That is a wonderful sign. Of course, the honest ones will admit that they don't like being there, but they also know how they came to be there in the first place.

In some instances, I have been allowed to take kids

to lunch and speak freely with them. It can be very telling, and it has frequently given me great insights into their particular program, including specific details on how well it works (or not). In these sessions, we do get a mix of the good, the bad, and the ugly, which allows us to sift through it with a balanced view.

I believe that it is very important to listen to the kids, just as it is important to listen to the staff. Nowadays when I am visiting a program on behalf of P.U.R.E. and come across a child who has a legitimate complaint, I will take a step that the casual parent-visitor may not; I'll attempt to resolve it by bringing it to the attention of the owner or director. I can tell a great deal more about the program if I get a negative or defensive response from a person in authority after I have raised the issue.

7. Inspect the kitchen and dining facilities. Lunch or laundry—what's that smell? Take a tour of the kitchen. The general cleanliness and orderliness (or lack thereof) can be a good indication of the standards that the program sets for the entire campus.

There's no point in pulling punches here—I get nosy. I open refrigerators, cabinets, and go through

pantries. As a visiting parent, you will probably not
have the ability to do that, so I make it a point to use
my privilege as a representative of P.U.R.E. to push the
boundaries on behalf of the families. I want to see food
that is stored in a sanitary way. It is not only vital to be
assured that the kids are fed well, but it is imperative
that they are eating food that is being prepared with
the proper attention to cleanliness and careful food
handling. There is a twofold benefit to that. On the one
hand, you get the assurance of reasonable food storage,
handling, and quality. On the other, you see the kids
who are on kitchen duty, learning the tasks and
procedures there. When they learn to cook something
well, how to properly handle food, how to manage
large amounts of food supplies, and how to deal with
a large outflow of trash and garbage, all the while
maintaining a clean work environment around
themselves, they are developing an adult sense of
responsibility as well as a set of real-world job skills.

It's great when you do an inspection and the news is
good. We visited one program for P.U.R.E. where they
baked fresh bread every morning! The smell permeated
the school. It was simply wonderful. Imagine a kid who,

only a few weeks earlier, had no saleable job skills, but who is now helping to manufacture such wonderful stuff every day. When you learn to bake in a commercial kitchen, you not only have a job skill that can be used almost anywhere but you have gained a personal understanding of the dignity of work and glean a sense of accomplishment and increased self-esteem from it.

8. Assess the academic program. What is their academic environment like? It may surprise you to learn that I do not expect top academic training from such a place, and I encourage parents to abandon thoughts of some sort of scholastic training camp. It is true that your child is going away to learn, but the truly important issues are emotional and psychological in nature. They simply are not matters of rigorous book work. Therefore, rather than holding the program up to the standards of the more desirable schools in the outside world, I look for a solid, basic learning environment where reasonable effort is made to keep the child on track with his or her ongoing school work.

Many parents start out this process thinking that if they are going to send Junior away, why not bring him home college-ready? They need to realize that until a child is out of the belligerent mode and adopts a sustained commitment to functional behavior, rigorous academic study will not benefit them. I have listened to some parents tell me what a high IQ their child has, or how talented, how athletic, how good-hearted they are. They often tell me these things to justify their concern for finding a class-A academic school that is magically combined with a disciplined and therapeutic residential program. I usually interrupt at that point and remind them to get their eyes back onto the ball.

If the state of a child's behavior has deteriorated to the point that he or she is using dangerous drugs, showing belligerent behavior to authority, making verbal threats against others, and expressing anger in unacceptable ways, how can stringent academics offer any value? Until a troubled child is returned to a reasonable level of emotional stability, they seldom have any interest in school. It fails to engage them, no matter how smart they are. Their degree of inner turmoil is such that to expect them to sustain academic excellence is like expecting them to appreciate the music of a symphony played in the middle of a howling windstorm.

Guarantees with Residential Therapy Programs

No program can *guarantee* specific results.

What are the guarantees in *life*? All we have is the *opportunity* to find faith and hope within ourselves that the changes our child undergoes in Residential Therapy will be good and lasting, and that our parent/child relationship will benefit from them for as long as we are in this life.

I do believe that your teen can learn enough to take him successfully into his future so that when the bumps and stumbles of life occur, he will be *far* better equipped to handle them. I suppose that the closest anyone is going to get to a guarantee is that if the program is valid, and if your child makes the effort, then he or she will return home with the tools of resiliency—to endure the slips and falls of life—and, most of all, to learn from the experience each time.

We measure a program's success by asking ourselves whether our troubled child could have achieved that prior to attending their specialty program. For all of the training and certification that it takes to run one of these programs, the purpose must always be to build up every child by training him with a network of functional social behaviors and by encouraging him to believe in himself so that when he inevitably falls down in life, he will know how to pick himself up, while keeping his momentary failures in perspective.

If we can offer our struggling teens an opportunity to find themselves again, the long and difficult journey will have been worth the effort. We can't look for guarantees; the staff and the students are all human and fallible. But as parents, we can take pride in knowing that during this vital transitory time of our teens' lives, we have taken every available step to help them build a future—and a self—of which they can be deservingly proud.

Appendix

About Parents' Universal Resource Experts (P.U.R.E.)

Parents' Universal Resource Experts, Inc. (P.U.R.E.) was founded in 2001 by Sue Scheff. For the past several years, P.U.R.E. has assisted families with valuable information and resources for their children and teens who are struggling with today's peer pressure, experimenting with drugs and alcohol, and simply good kids starting to make bad choices. P.U.R.E. has many very satisfied families that have used its services. Please take a moment to read some of their testimonials on www.helpyourteens.com.

Whether you are seeking Boarding Schools, Therapeutic Boarding Schools, Residential Treatment Centers, Wilderness Programs, Christian Boarding Schools, Summer Programs, Military Schools or other options, P.U.R.E. can help educate you in this very important decision for your child and family. We invite you to fill out a request form on our website for more information.

P.U.R.E is about *parents helping parents*. As a parent who experienced and *survived* a difficult teen, Sue Scheff designed her organization with the realization that desperate parents are at high risk of making rash and detrimental decisions in choosing the best placement for their child.

Doctors, attorneys, therapists, police departments, schools, guidance counselors, and other professionals refer families to P.U.R.E. In many cases, after a family has used our service, they recommend us to their friends and relatives. We have built our reputation on trust and putting families first.

In searching for schools and programs, we look for the following:

- Helping teens—not harming them.

- Building them up—not breaking them down.

- Positive and nurturing environments—
  not punitive.

- Family involvement in programs—not isolation
  from the teen.

- Protect children—not punish them.

As a member of the Better Business Bureau for many years, P.U.R.E. prides itself on helping others and *bringing families back together*.

Index

About the Author

About the Author

Sue Scheff is a Parent Advocate who founded Parents' Universal Resources Experts, Inc. (P.U.R.E.) in January 2001. Originally from Pleasant Valley,

Sue Scheff with her daughter, Ashlyn

New York, she relocated to Florida in 1985 with her family. Since 2001 she has devoted her time, energy, and support to helping parents find healthy and safe environments for their children. This happened after she, as a single mother of two, experienced the turmoil her own teenage daughter faced. Feeling alone and hopeless, Scheff researched the Internet seeking guidance and was directed into a program that misrepresented their organization in the worst way. This type of marketing proved very detrimental. "There is not a situation *that* desperate that could risk your child being placed into a children's prison disguised as a specialty school."

This is what gives Sue her strong desire to help families find *safe, qualified* placement, as well as *healthy* placement. P.U.R.E. was created for a need of "Parent Awareness" or

"Buyer's Beware" in a DESPERATE situation. P.U.R.E.'s motto is *"bringing families back together,"* not misrepresenting them.

Sue Scheff has been featured on *20/20, The Rachael Ray Show, ABC News i-Caught, Fox Morning Show with Mike and Juliet, Canadian CBC Sunday News Magazine, CNN Headline News, Fox News, KFI Talk Radio with John and Ken, BBC Talk Radio,* and *NPR,* discussing topics of Internet defamation as well as her work helping troubled teens through her organization. Further she has appeared in many national and international print articles, including *USA Today, Wall Street Journal, Washington Post, Miami Herald, Sun Sentinel, Asian Tribune, San Francisco Chronicle, Forbes, Capital Journal, Brazilian Veja, Washington Times, South Florida Parenting, Silicon Valley Business Journal,* and *South Florida Business Journal.*

You can visit Sue Scheff at www.suescheff.com or through her organization's site www.helpyourteens.com.

———

Ashlyn graduated from United Stuntmens Association–International Stunt School in 2005 and is a Certified Stuntwoman as well as a Certified Gymnastics Coach. Gymnastics is still her passion. She is pursuing her career in coaching gymnastics and works with many young girls in the area.